BY THE SHORE

SHORE

Explore the
Pacific Northwest Coast
Like a Local

NANCY BLAKEY

Photographs by Nick Hall
Illustrations by Teresa Grasseschi

 SASQUATCH BOOKS
SEATTLE

In memory of my father who moved his protesting family to the Pacific Northwest

Contents

WINTER

SPRING

Introduction

Many years ago at a retreat I met a woman from the East Coast. When I told her where I was from, her eyes widened.

"Bainbridge Island? The back door of the Olympic Mountains? I went hiking in the Olympics last year on vacation and I still dream of that trip. You must hike and paddle all the time."

I was taken aback. The truth was, the extent of my regular outdoor time was walking the dog around the neighborhood. I mumbled something and we parted, but she had planted a seed.

I came home and saw the mountains across Puget Sound, the islands and beaches beckoning through her eyes, and asked myself, Why didn't I hike more? Why didn't I plan a Sunday afternoon at the beach or fish for those beautiful salmon treading water outside my back door? I had no excuse; I have always loved the outdoors. Somehow it had slid away with the kids and work and the never-ending list of things to do. But suddenly I wanted to own and honor the place the woman from the East Coast dreamed about; I wanted to know it intimately. I joined REI and bought two small kayaks and a backpack. I began to plan local outdoor excursions instead of assuming the magical day would arrive when I had the time and everything lined up to go. I didn't wait for the weather and bought good rain gear and a Discover Pass for Washington State Parks. Over the years I was struck by the elation I felt exploring, even through storms or under a lid of gray skies. I found that science backed up that lift.

"Imagine a therapy that had no known side effects, was readily available, and could improve your cognitive functioning at zero cost."

This is the striking opening sentence of a University of Michigan study that found that time spent outdoors made people sharper and more creative thinkers. Other studies related to time spent outdoors had similar findings:

· Trouble sleeping? Go outside.
· Stressed? Go outside.
· Need more energy? Go outside.
· Want to elevate your mood? Go outside.

Research is proving we need the great outdoors for more than fresh air. We need it to become happier, healthier human beings, and you have in your hands a book of ideas to make that happen. We are in Pacific Northwest paradise, where the waters teem with seafood the rest of the world pays big bucks for, which is yours with a license. There are lighthouses, seaside bike paths, and uninhabited islands to explore. You may get lost or sunburned. You may skin your knees like a kid. You may detour somewhere unexpected, but that may lead you into a bigger life.

In our ever-increasingly indoor lives, you will have to plan to make it happen. Do it. You will not regret it. The best memories are made when we ask, Why not? Look at a map. Pick a trip or activity, a project or recipe. Take advantage of the Pacific Northwest's gorgeous coast. It could change everything.

P A C I F I

①

BRITISH COLUMBIA

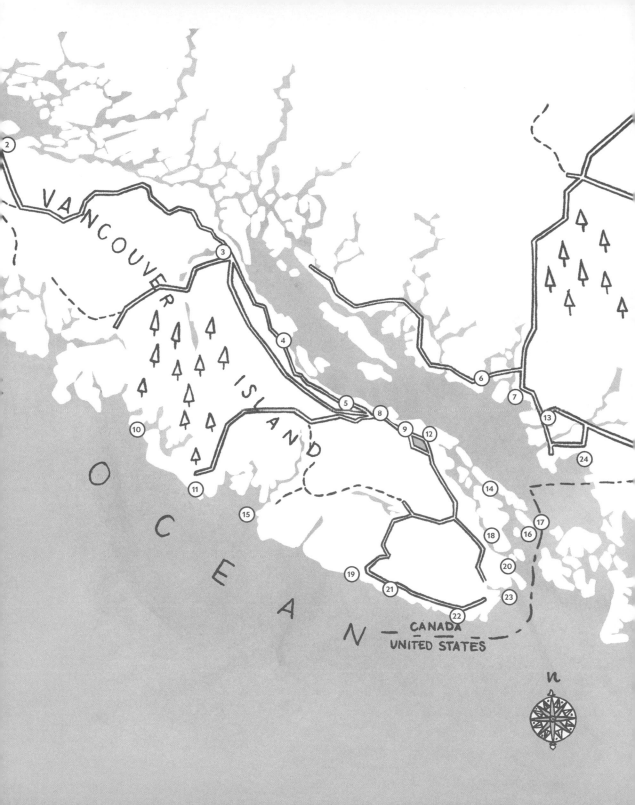

WASHINGTON

1 Blaine
2 Bellingham
3 Orcas Island
4 San Juan Island
5 Lopez Island
6 Anacortes/Guemes Island
7 La Conner
8 Camano Island
9 Port Townsend
10 Whidbey Island
11 Sequim
12 Port Angeles/Olympic Discovery Trail
13 Neah Bay
14 Cape Flattery
15 Shi Shi Beach
16 Forks
17 La Push
18 One Square Inch of Silence/ Hoh Rain Forest
19 Everett
20 Point No Point Lighthouse
21 Kingston
22 Edmonds
23 Bainbridge Island
24 Hood Canal/Dosewallips State Park
25 Seattle
26 Vashon Island
27 Des Moines
28 Port Orchard
29 Blake Island
30 Federal Way
31 Gig Harbor
32 Tacoma
33 Hope Island
34 Olympia
35 Kalaloch
36 Moclips
37 Copalis Beach
38 Ocean Shores
39 Westport
40 Long Island
41 Long Beach/ Discovery Trail
42 Ilwaco

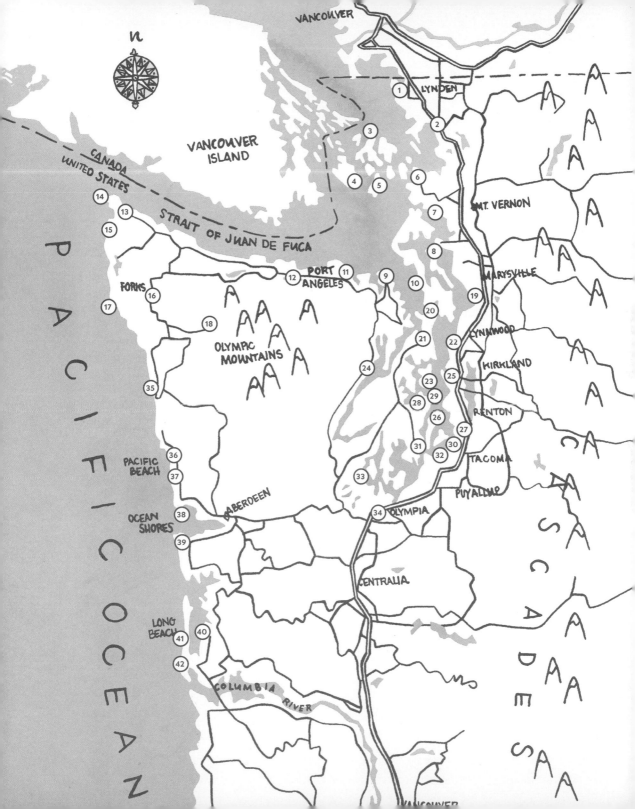

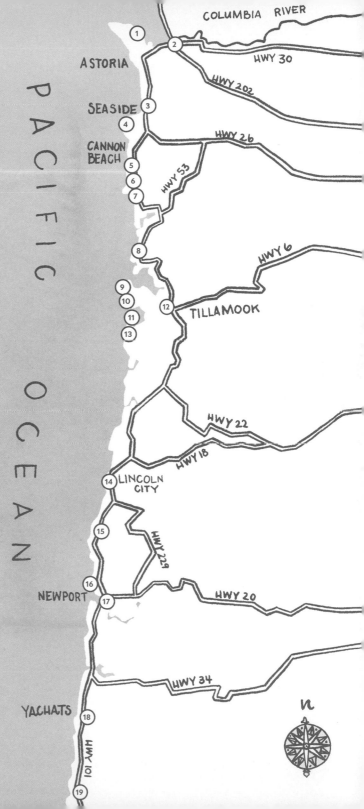

COLUMBIA RIVER

HWY 30

HWY 202

ASTORIA

SEASIDE

HWY 26

CANNON BEACH

HWY 53

HWY 6

TILLAMOOK

HWY 22

HWY 18

LINCOLN CITY

HWY 229

NEWPORT

HWY 20

HWY 34

YACHATS

HWY 101

PACIFIC OCEAN

n

SUMMER

Outings

WHALE-WATCHING TRIPS IN THE SALISH SEA

The Salish Sea is one of the world's largest and most biologically rich inland seas. Transcending borders and man-made territory divisions, it stretches from Desolation Sound north of Vancouver, Canada, through the coastal waterways of Puget Sound, all the way south to the city of Olympia in Washington. It is a single ecosystem where a wide variety of whales feed on the marine sea life, and when we think of whale watching in the Pacific Northwest, we usually think of the striking orca, or killer whale.

Resident orcas of the Salish Sea feed on salmon. In winter when the salmon numbers decrease, the pods head out to the open North Pacific Ocean to hunt. As the salmon return to the Salish Sea to spawn from April through early October, the orcas follow, giving us greater opportunities for sightings. These resident orca pods are not to be confused with transient orcas, which feed on sea mammals, not fish. Transients are sometimes called the "wolves of the sea" for their highly organized and fierce hunting techniques. Sightings of both resident and transient orcas are concentrated from the Strait of Juan de Fuca to the San Juan and Gulf Islands, with appearances of minke, gray, and humpback whales also possible during the summer.

The Whale Trail (TheWhaleTrail.org) organization highlights a series of sites from Vancouver Island to the Oregon coast where you can view whales from shore. You could get lucky in August and encounter a pod while aboard a ferry or from the shore, but to increase your chances, take a whale-watching excursion and let the experts guide you.

Vancouver Island

The best chance for encountering orcas near Vancouver Island is from the small towns of **Telegraph Cove** and **Port McNeil** in the Northeast, a 6-hour drive from Victoria and well worth the effort. There is one whale-watching operator out of Telegraph Cove, Stubbs Island Whale Watching, but also consider viewing whales by kayak with the highly rated North Island Kayak Company (NorthIslandKayak.ca). It also offers a multiday trip to experience

TYPES OF WHALES YOU ARE LIKELY
TO SEE IN THE PACIFIC NORTHWEST

Orca | SIZE: 16 TO 26 FEET

Orcas are a toothed whale and the largest member of the dolphin family. They have the dolphin's high intelligence and tight family structure, and they inhabit every ocean on earth although they are more abundant in cooler waters like the Salish Sea. Unlike other whales that follow an established migration route, orcas follow the food. Resident orcas feed mainly on salmon while transient orcas live in smaller pods and feed on sea mammals.

Gray | SIZE: 45 TO 48 FEET

Grays are large coastal whales that can grow up to 55 feet long. They migrate over 9,000 miles round-trip along the Pacific Coast from the Baja California Peninsula, Mexico, to their feeding grounds in Alaska, then back again. There is a small but growing population of grays that spends the summer in the Salish Sea to forage for invertebrates in the rich sediment on the sea bottom.

Minke | SIZE: 22 TO 24 FEET

Though smallest of the Salish Sea baleen whales, minkes are the most numerous of the baleen type. They tend to be solitary but sometimes gather together in small pods to feed and forage. They are often recognized at sea by their snout-first surfacing and their small, weak blows. Minke calves have a short lactation period and are usually weaned before their summer arrival in the Salish Sea, making them rarely seen beside their mother.

Humpback | SIZE: 40 TO 60 FEET

Humpbacks are occasional visitors to the Salish Sea as they migrate along the Pacific Coast to Mexico and Hawaii to give birth. Males are the Luciano Pavarottis of the whale world and create haunting songs that can last nearly half an hour. The average humpback devours between 4,500 and 5,500 pounds of krill, plankton, and small schooling fish during the feeding season.

more of the abundant marine wildlife in the area—Dall's porpoises, sea lions, and dolphins; the trip includes camping out on stunning local islands for memories that will last into the dark of winter.

Victoria has several whale-excursion companies on the harbor seafront within walking distance of the Black Ball Ferry terminal with Prince of Whales Whale Watching (PrinceOfWhales.com), a local favorite. On-demand tours are available; just show up and sign up according to your schedule.

The city of **Sidney**, accessed by Washington State Ferries from Anacortes, also has fine orca viewing. The water is calmer around Sidney due to the protection of the Gulf Islands, so this may be a better whale-watching option for small children and those prone to seasickness.

Campbell River during the salmon season is one of my favorite places on Vancouver Island (see Road Trip: Victoria to Campbell River, page 21). Campbell River Whale Watching and Adventure Tours (CampbellRiverWhaleWatching.com) offers whale tours that have opportunities for viewing other marine wildlife on the same trip. Best of all, you can combine whale watching with salmon fishing afterward on the Campbell River public pier.

San Juan Islands

The **San Juan Islands** offer a wide variety of excellent whale excursions. You can go by sailboat, kayak, Zodiac (inflatable motorboat), or cruiser with covered cabins to protect you from inclement weather. Your best bet for finding a tour to suit your needs is to check out the list at the San Juan Islands Visitors Bureau website (VisitSanJuans.com) for operators on each island. Washington State Ferries sailings leave Anacortes for Lopez, San Juan, Shaw, and Orcas Islands with multiple daily departures. Reservations are recommended in the summer months (bit.ly/1BB4C1U).

All of the San Juan Islands whale-tour operators sail the same waters and radio one another when a sighting occurs. Your chances of seeing whales are equal from each island. The predominant whales in the San Juan Islands in summer are the southern resident orcas, and one of the world's best places to see orcas from dry land is Lime Kiln Point State Park on the west side of San Juan Island. This 36-acre park also has a meandering walk to a picturesque lighthouse open for tours during summer. A reader board there lists the latest whale sightings. There is also an interpretive center at Lime Kiln. Pack a picnic, binoculars, and sunscreen for a lovely day of whale watching, then camp out at nearby San Juan County Park, build a fire, and watch the sunset. Make reservations! It is a popular place. FYI: Hammock tents are not allowed.

Be sure to visit the Whale Museum (WhaleMuseum.org) in **Friday Harbor** on San Juan Island. It has maps to guide you to places where you can whale watch from the shore, and if you choose to view them by sea, staff can make recommendations for tour operators in the area. You can also learn about the devastating effects of noise pollution on whales and listen to each type of whale's haunting call in a cool little phone booth.

Puget Sound

Seattle may be a convenient place to launch from for whale watching, but Elliott Bay does not have the abundance of sightings that northern Puget Sound has. Clipper Vacations (ClipperVacations.com) offers whale-watching tours that leave from downtown Seattle for a day trip north to the **San Juan Islands**, where most whale sightings are. It is a 12-hour tour, and after whale watching there is a stopover in **Friday Harbor** to eat lunch or explore.

Out of **Edmonds**, north of Seattle, you can take the Puget Sound Express tour (PugetSoundExpress.com) on a catamaran hydrofoil that cruises up to 50 miles per hour. It will get into more fertile whale-watching territory in a jiffy. Two more reasons to pick Puget Sound Express: homemade blueberry cake is served, and a whale sighting is guaranteed or your next trip is free. It is family owned and operated.

Anacortes and **Bellingham** have multiple tour operators that also cruise to the San Juan Islands, where the orcas are feeding, without the expense of a ferry ride to the islands.

In **Port Townsend** Puget Sound Express wins again in my book by offering both daylong whale-watching expeditions and a passenger ferry between Port Townsend and Friday Harbor from May through September. You can bring your kayak or bicycle on board for a small fee and reserve a return trip on the boat a few days later.

Oregon Coast

The **Oregon coast** is famous for its gray-whale migration from mid-December to mid-January as nearly twenty thousand of them move south from Alaska to the warmer waters of the Baja California Peninsula in Mexico to give birth. Then, from late March to June, they migrate north along the coast on their

UNDERSTANDING TIDES

Tides are important for everything from coastal navigation to recreational shellfish harvesting on beaches, and understanding them is a part of living by the shore. A tide is the cyclic rising and falling of the earth's oceans generated by the gravitational pull of the moon and sun. There are several factors that affect tides: the position of the sun and moon relative to earth, the rotation of the earth itself, and the local bathymetry (topography) of the ocean floor. Strong winds and heavy rain can also affect the height of tides. In simple terms, high tide is the height in feet of the highest point of the tide on any given shore, and low tide is the lowest height. The period between a tidal change from high to low or low to high is known as slack tide, and slack water time varies from day to day, particularly on full or new moons, which is why the tide times in the Pacific Northwest change every day. There are generally three types of tides: diurnal (one high tide and one low tide per day), semidiurnal (two equal high tides and two equal low tides per day), and mixed semidiurnal (two unequal high tides and two unequal low tides per day). Here in the Pacific Northwest, we have mixed semidiurnal tides, with tide times moving approximately 50 minutes ahead each day.

How to Read a Tide Table

A tide table is a valuable resource for learning not only when the tides will be high and low, but what the height of each will be. For example, you need a minus tide (a tide below the average low-water mark) to gather oysters. A local tide table for the beach you want to harvest at will give you information on the height of the low tides, including the time of the minus tides needed for harvesting. Even though tide tables may be formatted differently, they all have the information you need: the date, the time of the tides, and their height in meters or feet. The height of the tides is measured against a defined plane of reference called "chart datum," an average of low-tide heights for the area that the tide table references as a 0 (zero) tide. The high tide is always the largest height of water on the beach above the chart datum. If the table says high tide will be 6 feet, then the water will be 6 feet above the average low-water mark of the area. Low tides are the smaller number in the tide table, sometimes a negative number if the ebb is below the chart datum. If you see a minus sign before the height of the low tide, it means the low tide is below the average low-water mark of the area. Tide-Forecast.com has an excellent and easy-to-read tide table for anywhere in the world; just enter your location.

Tide Terms

- **EBB TIDE:** The tide going out away from shore, to low tide
- **FLOOD TIDE:** The tide moving in toward shore, to high tide
- **HIGH TIDE:** When the tide is at its greatest water elevation, also known as high water and often signified by "HW" in a tide table
- **INTERTIDAL ZONE:** The slice of seashore exposed at low tide and covered at high tide; a rich ecosystem for marine life
- **LOW TIDE:** When the tide is at its lowest water elevation, often signified as LW in a tide table
- **MEAN HIGH WATER (MHW):** The average high-water height taken over a period of years
- **MEAN LOW WATER (MLW):** The average low-water height taken over a period of years
- **MINUS TIDE:** An unusually low tide below the chart datum (0 feet), the average low tide for the area

- **NEAP TIDE:** Tides that occur during or near the first and last quarters of the moon, causing a decreased range of tidal movement
- **RIPTIDE:** A strong current caused by tidal flow pulling toward the sea
- **SPRING TIDE:** Tides that occur twice a month during the new and full moon when the earth, sun, and moon are closely aligned. Their collective gravitational pull causes higher high tides and lower low tides
- **TIDAL CURRENT:** The water current caused by tides
- **TIDAL RANGE:** The difference in depth between high and low tide, important information when navigating by boat
- **ZERO TIDE HEIGHT:** The chart datum of an area; an average height of all the low tides that determines the zero reference that the tides will be measured against

way to feed in Alaska. In the summer there are a small number of resident grays that feed near **Depoe Bay**, a 2.5-hour drive from Portland. These resident grays do not migrate to Alaska but instead stay around the shoreline near Depoe Bay to feed and fatten. There is a whale-watching center in Depoe Bay with a viewing platform. Use the resource Whale Watching Spoken Here (bit.ly/1C8DScA) to guide you on the migrating gray whales of the Pacific Coast. For more, see Spring Whale Watch Week in Oregon on page 216.

KAYAK CAMPING TRIPS

There are hundreds of excellent kayak rental places in the Pacific Northwest that will teach you the paddling fundamentals and take you on multiday campouts to dazzling islands and beaches. Given tidal currents, wind, and the dynamic nature of sea conditions, a guided tour is an excellent way to get you started out on the water.

Blake Island | *2 days*

If you're already adept at kayaking and ready to try a self-guided trip, try a slow paddle through **Seattle's Elliott Bay** to **Blake Island**. Watch the weather forecast; if it calls for a series of quintessentially calm summer days, you do not need to be an expert paddler for this trip. North winds can pick up in the afternoon; however, the mornings are usually calm. The island is a few miles from Seattle and a world away in time. A midweek campout on the island makes a stunning summer getaway, as the crowds have thinned and the beaches are empty but for the raccoons pawing through seaweed for clams at low tide.

What makes Blake Island special is its designation for marine camping only: you must arrive by boat. There are forty-four campsites that line the sandy beach, with most of them facing west, perfect for watching our famous Northwest summer sunsets. Paddle to the west side of the island to reach the campsites. All the campsites have fire rings; bring your own firewood or buy it from the small store on the island, open summer months only. Burning driftwood is not allowed. You could also try to catch your dinner. Crabbing and clamming are popular here.

SILVERDALE

HWY 303

SHILSHOLE BAY

DISCOVERY PARK

DYES INLET

PORT ORCHARD BAY

BAINBRIDGE ISLAND

MURDEN COVE

⑦

CREOSOTE

HWY 303

⑧

PUGET SOUND

HWY 3

SINCLAIR INLET

③ MANCHESTER

⑥

PORT ORCHARD

COLBY

① BLAKE ISLAND

⑤

WES SEAT

② ④

BLAKE ISLAND

1 Blake Island Northwest Campsite
2 Southworth Put-In
3 Manchester Put-In
4 Vashon Island Put-In
5 Lincoln Park Put-In
6 Alki Beach Put-In
7 Eagle Harbor Put-In
8 Fort Ward Put-In

VASHON ISLAND

VASHON HWY

N

Access Put-Ins and Paddle Distances
- **BAINBRIDGE ISLAND:** Eagle Harbor, 6 miles; Fort Ward State Park, 2.5 miles
- **WEST SEATTLE:** Lincoln Park, 3.5 miles; Alki Beach Park, 4 miles
- **PORT ORCHARD:** Southworth/Vashon ferry terminal, 1 mile; Manchester State Park, 2 miles
- **VASHON ISLAND:** North ferry terminal, 1.5 miles

Kayak Rentals or Guided Tours
- **BAINBRIDGE ISLAND:** Back of Beyond, TotheBackofBeyond.com
- **WEST SEATTLE:** Alki Kayak Tours, KayakAlki.com
- **VASHON ISLAND:** Vashon Watersports, VashonWatersports.com

What to Bring in Addition to Your Camping Gear

KAYAK GEAR:
- Neoprene gloves
- Water shoes for kayaking
- Personal flotation device for each paddler
- Map of your route and map of the island (download at bit.ly/2rLJDtd)
- Spray skirt
- Heavy-duty garbage bags or dry bags for stowing your gear into the holds
- Flare and/or whistle

PERSONAL GEAR:
- Binoculars for viewing marine wildlife
- Small dry bag for your cell phone
- Firewood
- Wicking (noncotton) layers
- Warm hat and/or sun hat
- Sunglasses and sunscreen
- Backpacker's camp chair for lounging on the beach and watching the sunset
- Shoes to hike 8 miles of trails on the island if desired

More Kayak Campouts: British Columbia

Keats Island | 3 days | Approximately 3 miles one way
Breathtaking **Howe Sound**, the location of **Keats Island**, is North America's southernmost fjord. The sound is often used as a setting for movie and television productions because its wild steep-sided beauty and the archipelago of islands scattered across it are a mere 13 miles northwest from the city of Vancouver and easily accessed by BC Ferry from Horseshoe Bay. Keats Island is an ideal place to paddle to and use as a base for exploring Howe Sound for several days. To begin the adventure, drive to **Horseshoe Bay** in west Vancouver and take the 20-minute ferry to **Bowen Island**. If you plan on renting kayaks, Bowen Island Sea Kayaking (bit.ly/2tv7Bh5) is next to the ferry terminal on the island and offers rentals, guided trips, and classes. They will help you tie the kayaks onto the car and give you directions for the 5.5-mile drive to **Turnstall Bay**, where you will park and launch the kayaks. From Turnstall Bay, paddle northwest for nearby Pasley Island and its necklace of small islands to explore. Nearby Ragged Island is a great place for a picnic, but no camping is allowed. Your destination is Plumper Cove Marine Provincial Park (bit.ly/2sWB2al) on the upper northwest side of Keats Island. When you arrive you will see the public wharf. Camping is allowed on beaches on Keats Island, but the park has water available and hiking trails that follow the coast and go into the forest. Make camp and spend the next few days exploring the clear waters and multiple islands of Howe Sound before heading back to Turnstall Bay. For a map of Howe Sound, visit bit.ly/2rJ6oib.

More Kayak Campouts: Washington

Hope Island | 2 days | ⅔ mile one way
Looking for a short paddle through tranquil water? If you put in at **Arcadia Point**, a 30-minute drive from **Olympia**, you will have less than a mile's paddle to this jewel of an island. **Hope Island** is also part of the Cascadia Marine Trail (see page 15), and access is by boat only. It is often empty of people except for the caretaker who lives there year round, and it is possible to have the island nearly to yourself. Paddle to the southwest side for the campsites. There are kayak racks there to keep your boat safely above the

high-tide line. Bring your own water (there is no fresh water available) and beach fires are not allowed, but the trade-off is bliss, solitude, and a night under the stars. For a map and more information, visit bit.ly/2qNKuw8.

CASCADIA MARINE TRAIL

Ready for an adventure? The Cascadia Marine Trail is a 150-mile inland sea trail extending from the **Canadian border** south through the **San Juan Islands** to the city of **Olympia** in south Puget Sound. The trail accesses a winding network of road ends, rest stops, marinas, and over sixty beach campsites designated for nonmotorized boaters only. There are quiet campsites on uninhabited islands like **Blake Island** (see page 10) or campsites in small towns, such as **Oak Harbor**, that have coffee shops and cafés. Look for clay babies on **Fox Island**—weird matrices of soil and salt water shaped by the tides into sweet round figures—or visit the Port Townsend Marine Science Center (PTMSC.org) and listen for whales on the hydrophone. You can experience the water trail on long open-water stretches or short day-trip paddles; the beauty of the trail is you can choose according to your time, energy, and level of experience. Many paddlers and sailors take several summers to work their way along the Cascadia Marine Trail. For more information and a list of organizations and clubs that participate in paddles on the trail, visit bit.ly/2rLJia7.

Long Island | *3 days* | *2 miles one way*
Long Island is the longest estuarine island on the Pacific Coast and is a wonderland of recreational opportunities. You can hunt for clams for your dinner at low tide on the west side of the island, hike through old-growth cedar forests, and explore this uninhabited island by foot or paddle. Bring your own kayak for this extraordinary trip or rent one in nearby **Raymond** at Willapa Paddle Adventures (bit.ly/2smjRRd), which also offers a drop-off and pickup service.

Pay attention to the tides on Long Island—the campsites are accessible only at high tide; when it goes out, the mudflats leave you stranded. Launch from the Willapa Bay National Wildlife Refuge boat launch near milepost 24 along US Highway 101; it is an easy paddle to the first campsite: Pinnacle Rock Campground, the closest and southernmost campsite on the island from the boat launch. Head from the boat launch toward the southern end of the island, paddle around the point, and the campsite is the first on the western shore. There is a total of five campsites and over twenty spaces available on the island on a first-come, first-served basis, each with a picnic table and a fire ring. Campers are advised to bring their own water. For a map, visit bit.ly/2u4goUu.

BEACH CAMPING TRIPS

A wide sky, pounding surf, tide pools, and stacks of driftwood set beach camping trips apart from classic mountain hikes, and summer is the ideal time to plan one.

Ocean-Side Hike and Campout at Shi Shi Beach | *3 days*
You can feel the sky getting bigger as you approach **Shi Shi Beach** (say "Shy-Shy") from the trail. When you reach the bluff and the seascape unfolds before you, pause and drink it in. Words like "epic" and "breathtaking" will rattle around in your head, but they do not do justice to this wild portion of the Pacific Coast. You are at the receiving end of the best the Pacific Northwest has to offer: a remote stretch of sandy beach, sea stacks, stars to gaze at come night, tide pools rich with marine life, and the Pacific Ocean in all its majesty.

When to Go
Shi Shi Beach can get crowded on weekends in the summer. If you have the luxury of planning your getaway midweek, you will have more solitude. Early autumn is also a good time for this hiking trip.

How to Get There
It is a long haul from **Seattle** to reach the Shi Shi trailhead, around 5 hours including the ferry ride to **Bainbridge Island**.

   Port Angeles is a 1.5-hour drive from the Bainbridge Island ferry dock. When arriving in Port Angeles, stop at the Olympic National Park Visitor Center to pick up a wilderness camping permit and a bear canister for

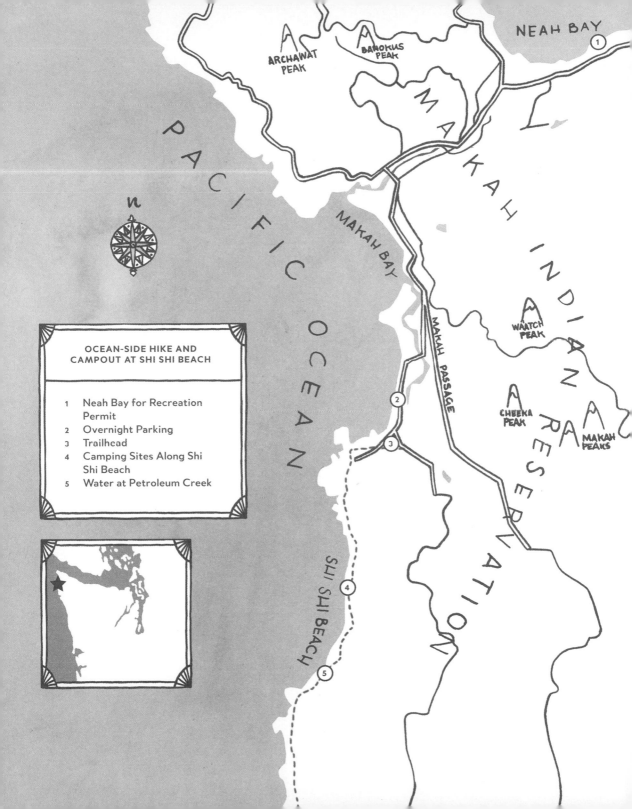

NEAH BAY

1

ARCHAWAT PEAK

BAHOKUS PEAK

M A K A H

MAKAH BAY

MAKAH PASSAGE

I N D I A N

WAATCH PEAK

CHEEKA PEAK

MAKAH PEAKS

R E S E R V A T I O N

PACIFIC OCEAN

n

2

3

SHI SHI BEACH

4

5

**OCEAN-SIDE HIKE AND
CAMPOUT AT SHI SHI BEACH**

1   Neah Bay for Recreation
    Permit
2   Overnight Parking
3   Trailhead
4   Camping Sites Along Shi
    Shi Beach
5   Water at Petroleum Creek

your food. The canisters are more for critters like raccoons than bears, and they are required for all overnight campers. Next stop, **Neah Bay**, where you can purchase a required recreation permit for parking on the Makah Reservation while you hike. Find the permit at several locations, including the Makah Marina (open until 5:00 p.m.) and the minimart (open until 10:00 p.m.). As with all coastal hikes, consulting a tide table is important to time your beach hike in order to not get stranded and have to wait for the tide to go out to reach your destination. Use the La Push/Quillayute River tide chart (bit.ly/2qPvgVn), and add 30 minutes for the tides at Shi Shi. For example, if low tide is at 10:30 a.m., add 30 minutes for the Shi Shi beach low tide: low tide will be at 11:00 a.m. See Understanding Tides on page 8 for more information.

There is no overnight parking allowed at the trailhead, so drop off your gear and fellow hikers, then drive back a half mile to a marked private home that offers parking to campers for $10 per day, cash only.

The 4-mile trail to the beach is not difficult, but it can be muddy in parts year round. There is a rope to help lower yourself a short distance down to the beach at the trail's end. Once you reach Shi Shi, there are many options for camping anywhere on the beach or at a few sites above the shore, with the beach the most popular. If you camp on the beach, make sure you set up camp above the high-tide watermark! There is water available from Petroleum Creek at the south end of the beach, but it must be boiled or treated.

Once you set up camp, build a beach fire and watch the sun set behind the stone arches and stacks. Other things to do while here: walk to Point of Arches and explore sea caves along the way, check out the tide pools at low tide, beachcomb or build driftwood forts, or simply breathe in the salt air from the crashing waves.

More Beach Camping Trips: British Columbia

Juan de Fuca Marine Trail | *5 days*
Located on the southwestern shore of **Vancouver Island**, this 30-mile hike stretches along a rugged rain-forest coastline with several ocean-side camps. The trail closely follows the coast along cliffs facing the Pacific, through rocky beaches and into second-growth forests. The Juan de Fuca Marine Trail is the southern extension of the wild West Coast Trail, and both finish in **Port Renfrew** from opposite directions. It is not an easy hike, but it is rewarding and you can shorten it to 11 miles by accessing it midtrail at Sombrio Beach or even to a 6.5-mile day hike from Parkinson Creek to Botanical Beach. If you do the full hike from China Beach to Port Renfrew, drop your pack on the porch of the Renfrew Pub (bit.ly/2u4dJdk) and reward yourself with a Fat Tug IPA—you deserve it! For more information on organizing the hike and arranging a bus pickup back to your car, visit JuandeFucaMarineTrail.com.

More Beach Camping Trips: Washington

Spencer Spit State Park | *3 days*
Spencer Spit is one of my top-five favorite state parks and has it all: on-the-water campsites, kayak rentals, driftwood for fort making, birds to watch, and a short but lovely hike along the spit. For a longer hike on Lopez Island, drive to the Iceberg Point trailhead. At the point, look for dried sea salt in the natural cups in the sandstone rocks and sprinkle it over clams bought from Jones Family Shellfish Farm (JFFarms.com/shellfish) and grilled on an open fire. Spencer Spit is popular; make reservations well in advance. For a map of Spencer Spit, visit bit.ly/2qIgUaY.

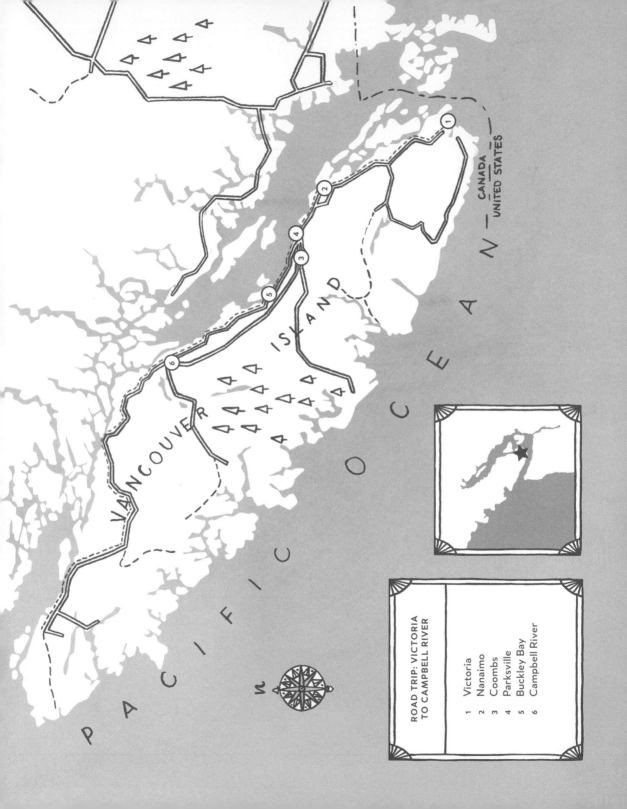

VANCOUVER ISLAND

PACIFIC OCEAN

CANADA
UNITED STATES

N

ROAD TRIP: VICTORIA
TO CAMPBELL RIVER

1   Victoria
2   Nanaimo
3   Coombs
4   Parksville
5   Buckley Bay
6   Campbell River

More Beach Camping Trips: Oregon

Cape Lookout | *3 days*

An easy 2-hour drive from Portland, Cape Lookout offers access to an expansive beach where you can put in miles of hiking, including a 2.5-mile walk to the headland that juts into the Pacific Ocean for a stunning overlook. If you are inclined to forego tent camping, you can also rent a cabin or a yurt here. Reservations are recommended (bit.ly/2qd9GrS); loops *C* and *D* are the most private of the campsite loops.

ROAD TRIP: VICTORIA TO CAMPBELL RIVER

Take New Zealand, limit the sheep, shrink it down in size, bring it to the Pacific Northwest, and you have **Vancouver Island**. Over 2,000 miles of coastline offer just about any outdoor adventure you can think of: kayaking, surfing, hiking, sailing, fishing, diving, and more. Most of the island is an outdoor enthusiast's mecca, but let's not forget the charmingly urbane city of **Victoria**, the gateway to the island, where you can provision your adventures with wild game salami, local brews, and (in my opinion) the world's best gingersnaps.

An exceptional August road trip runs for 165 miles from Victoria north to **Campbell River**; the king salmon are running and the farmers' markets are filled with the bounty of summer. It is a 4-hour drive straight through, but it is best to take your time, meander, detour to beaches and delis, stop to stare at goats on roofs, and hunt down Kusshi oysters. Begin the adventure by taking the Black Ball Ferry (CohoFerry.com) to Victoria out of Port Angeles, Washington State Ferries from Anacortes, or BC Ferries from Vancouver, British Columbia. The *Victoria Clipper* also makes daily runs from downtown Seattle, but it is passenger only (no cars).

Once you're in Victoria, the journey starts from downtown. Park the car in a lot near the ferry terminal and rent a bicycle for a few hours from the Pedaler (ThePedaler.ca), located across from the Black Ball Ferry terminal. You get a more intimate view of a city by bike and you won't have to struggle for parking. Among the dozens of worthy stops in downtown Victoria, there are three places not to miss. Choux Choux Charcuterie

(ChouxChouxCharc.com) specializes in European-style house-made pâtés, sausages, and artisanal cheeses, and with 24-hour notice the shop can make you a memorable gourmet picnic. Near Choux Choux is Crust Bakery (CrustBakery.ca), which has my idea of the perfect gingersnap cookie: crunchy on the outside, moist in the middle. Hop back on the bike with your stash and ride to the iconic store Capital Iron (CapitalIron.net). It's hard to find one word to describe this large, old-fashioned place—it is a hardware store, REI, and kitchen shop rolled together. You will find everything you forgot or need for your salmon fishing, surfing, and hiking adventures at incredibly reasonable prices. Buy an oyster-shucking knife; you'll need it later.

Return the bike, load up the car, and head north on BC Highway 1 to **Nanaimo**, home of the Nanaimo bar, a luscious layer of yellow custard sandwiched between rich chocolate ganache and a coconut-graham crust. Buy some of the best at Bocca Cafe (bit.ly/2t6KlmV). They also make delicious gluten-free Nanaimo bars. Explore Nanaimo or detour east on BC 4 to **Coombs**—a quirky little town of wooden buildings with grass roofs, where goats peer down at you with gimlet eyes like you are the weird one. Check out the eclectic Old Country Market (bit.ly/2tqw86C), then go behind the market and enjoy an outdoor Mexican lunch at Taqueria (bit.ly/2tk35xo). Buy ice cream cones at Coombs Ice Cream Parlor (bit.ly/2sslMyt) for dessert, and if you are traveling with kids, let them order the neon-blue bubble gum ice cream. It is worth a photo.

Say goodbye to the goats and head east on BC Highway 4A to the seaside community of **Parksville** and one of my favorite beaches on the island at Parksville Community Park. At low tide the ocean recedes over half a mile, leaving a wide expanse of sand and warm, shallow water calm enough for toddlers to splash in. Bring a picnic, a blanket, and if the kids are with you, tools for digging in the sand. If you are here between mid-July and mid-August, don't miss the sand castle exhibition (see Parksville Beach Festival, page 61). After beach time hit the spray park and use its water cannon for the kids to rinse off. This large park is not just family friendly; there are skate ramps and beach volleyball courts if you are inclined to join the locals and play.

After a long and leisurely beach time, get back in the car, head north up BC 19A, and start thinking about dinner: Fanny Bay and Kusshi oysters. Stop at **Buckley Bay**, where a ferry leaves for the vibrant islands of Hornby and Densmore. You can get gas, and behind the gas station is Fanny Bay

Oyster and Seafood Shop (bit.ly/2tv2j5i), where you will find local, farm-fresh oysters. Next stop, Campbell River.

Campbell River in August is filled with people fishing for the granddaddy of all salmon: the chinook (king) salmon. Walk the city pier and check out the folks fishing from the dock. This is one among many reasons why I love Campbell River: you do not need a guide or a fancy boat or your own equipment for salmon fishing. You can catch a 30-pound chinook from the pier and haul it up with special trap nets that are free for use by the public. There are also fish-cleaning stations with running water, and Ben Luck's concession stand on Discovery Pier has rod rentals: kids under 15 pay nothing and adults are charged $10 CAD for several hours of fishing, lures included. Get your fishing license online before you go (see Resources, page 223).

The best way to stay in Campbell River is to find a home or cabin through Vacation Rentals By Owner (VRBO.com). Find a place that suits your needs and budget, be it pets, large families, or a romantic place for two. In addition you will have a kitchen to prepare the salmon you catch.

Rise early to join locals to fish for the kings. Sunday is farmers' market day, right next to the public pier, and when you are done fishing, browse the abundance of local farms and artists. You can find honey, vine-ripened tomatoes, and big rocks split and polished into cheese platters, perfect for a holiday gift.

MICRO-ADVENTURE: RENT A TREE HOUSE

Get out, get up, and get away from it all in a tree house. The Pacific Northwest has multiple accommodations in the arms of a tree. For choices from cheap to chic, visit the Airbnb website (Airbnb.com) for the **Seattle** area and on **Lopez** and **Whidbey Islands**. For even more options, check out **Fall City**'s Tree House Point Resort (TreeHousePoint.com). **Vancouver Island**'s Free Spirit Spheres (FreeSpiritSpheres.com) is a unique tree house resort of beautiful and trippy spheres secured in the trees of a coastal rain forest.

Catch it, Cook it, Eat it

CLAMS

Dig for your dinner! Clams are a great source of protein and free of hormones and dyes, and they are ravishingly delicious grilled over an open fire and dipped in butter.

Where to Go

Unlike Puget Sound or the Pacific Coast, **Hood Canal** rarely has beach closures from paralytic shellfish poison (see Paralytic Shellfish Poison, page 27), particularly south of **Quilcene**, and for this reason Dosewallips State Park is the place to go for clam digging. It is a large and scenic park on Hood Canal with 5 miles of shoreline studded with clams and oysters. From the Bainbridge Island ferry dock, the drive is just over an hour. Manila and the native littleneck clams are abundant here, and you can dig your limit on the beach in a short amount of time. Gather friends and family and make it a clam fest by camping or staying in one of the rustic cabins at the park; cook the bounty on a campfire. For reservations, visit bit.ly/2qhQnxS.

More Clamming Beaches

There are hundreds of beaches to dig for clams up and down the Salish Sea. For a complete list from the Washington Department of Fish and Wildlife, visit bit.ly/2qTGd8w. The following is a short list of popular beaches and the types of clams most abundant there.

British Columbia
- **TOFINO**: Manila and littleneck clams
- **DEEPWATER BAY**: Manila and littleneck clams

Washington
- **BIRCH BAY STATE PARK**: Littleneck and manila clams
- **SEQUIM BAY STATE PARK**: Butter and native littleneck clams
- **INDIAN ISLAND COUNTY PARK**: Butter, manila, littleneck, horse clams, and geoducks below a minus-2-foot tide

Oregon
- **TILLAMOOK BAY**: Butter, cockle, and horse clams
- **NETARTS BAY**: Butter, cockle, and horse clams

Equipment
- Shellfish license (see Resources, page 223)
- *Handbook of Washington Sport Fishing Rules* (available free where you buy your license), *Oregon Sport Fishing Regulations* (bit.ly/2tv9mem), or BC's sport fishing guide (bit.ly/2tqafEL)
- Clam gauge, for measuring size (available at most sporting goods stores)
- One bucket per person digging (mixing clams between people is prohibited)
- Small hand rake or trowel
- Frozen cooler pack
- Rubber boots (or hip waders if desired—you will be walking and kneeling in muddy sand)

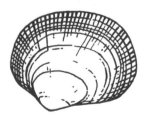 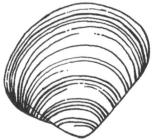

WARNING

Paralytic Shellfish Poison

Paralytic shellfish poison (PSP) is a naturally occurring biotoxin caused by algae blooms, sometimes called a red tide, that is filtered through mollusks, including clams. You cannot cook PSP out, and it can be fatal if you ingest affected shellfish. The biotoxin doesn't harm the shellfish but can climb to levels dangerous to humans until the bloom subsides and the clams flush it from their systems. PSP has always been around, and scientists are unsure of what causes the toxic blooms. In earlier centuries coastal tribes would rub a small piece of clam on the inner lip. If it tingled, there was PSP present. Today we have shellfish monitoring hotlines that will inform you if it is safe to dig, and it is critical to call before you hit the beach.

- For Washington beaches, call the Shellfish Safety Hotline at 1-800-562-5632.
- For Oregon, call the Oregon Department of Agriculture's Shellfish Safety Hotline: 1-800-448-2474.
- For British Columbia, visit bit.ly/U5b8ML or call the Red Tide Hotline: 1-866-431-3474.

Amnesic Shellfish Poisoning from Domoic Acid Toxicity

Like PSP, domoic acid (DA) is a naturally occurring biotoxin in algae blooms that can be ingested by shellfish, raising the acid in their flesh to dangerous levels for the humans who ingest them. The resulting illness from toxic levels of domoic acid is called amnesic shellfish poisoning. Domoic acid is found most frequently on the coast, the natural habitat of razor clams, making them the most affected shellfish, although a few scattered cases of DA have been detected in shellfish from Puget Sound. To be safe, always call the hotline numbers above for beach closures before digging.

Technique

You will need to dig for all shellfish at low tide (see page 8). For manila and littleneck clams, look for a "show"—small holes in the mud or gravel, often in a cluster. For horse clams, look for a hole that squirts a jet of water at you. Use the hand rake to dig several inches down and the manila or littleneck will appear; usually they are only 3 to 6 inches deep and you do not need to dig far to uncover them, while horse clams are up to 10 inches deep. Geoducks are the king of clams, but you can dig for them only on minus-2-foot tides. Use a regular-size shovel; they are buried 2 to 3 feet deep.

Measure the manila and littleneck clams with the gauge: they need to be at least 1.5 inches long at the widest distance across the shell to keep. You can also use a Sharpie to mark 1.5 inches on your bucket and measure against that. There are no minimum size restrictions for geoduck and horse clams. Be sure to fill the hole back up when you are done digging. Place the clams in seawater in your bucket as you collect them and keep the water cold by placing the frozen cooler pack inside.

Clams bought from the store are already purged, but it is a good idea to purge clams collected on the beach to get rid of the sand and grit they hold inside. To purge them, keep the clams in the bucket of seawater stored in a cool place for several hours. The rule of thumb is 4 hours, though many cooks do this overnight. Check them once in a while; they should have their siphons out, a good sign. After purging, you will see the sand collected at the bottom of the bucket. Rinse the clams, place them in a colander with a plate underneath, settle a wet dishcloth over them, and keep them in the refrigerator. The clams will keep up to 2 days. Be sure to discard clams that do not close when you tap them, and do *not* store live clams in a plastic bag or they will quickly die.

Types of Clams You Are Likely to Find

Native Littleneck Clams

A delicious clam also known as the steamer clam, the native littleneck is round to oval in shape with fine ridges that radiate both around and down the shell, with the pattern *across* the shell slightly more prominent than the pattern down the shell. They tend to be cream and gray and can grow to 4 inches wide. Littlenecks mature slowly and take 4 to 6 years to reach commercial size. You will find them 3 to 4 inches deep at midtide level typically in gravel mixed with rocks and mud in sheltered bays and tidal flats.

Manila Clams

Very similar in taste, size, and shape to the native littleneck, manilas are what you will find most commonly in supermarket seafood sections. The shells have darker patterns and are slightly more oval than round compared to littlenecks. They also have fine ridges, but the ridges tend to be slightly more prominent *down* the shell than across. Manilas can be found above the midtide level in gravel mixed with mud, rocks, and sand; in sheltered bays; and in tidal flats.

Horse (or Gaper) Clams

Horse clams, or fat gapers, have chalky white shells with a flared space to accommodate their siphon, which does not retract. They can grow up to 10 inches long, and at low tide you will see their spitting jets of water as you walk across the tide zone. Dig deep! Fat gapers live 12 to 16 inches down in a sand, mud, and gravel matrix in the lower tide zone.

Butter Clams

Butters are large, meaty clams considered the best clam for chowders. They are yellowish to light-ash colored with concentric rings and grow up to 5 inches wide. You will find butter clams in groups—where you find one, you will find more. Dig 8 to 14 inches down in lower intertidal or shallow subtidal zones in sand and gravel conditions. Butters can live up to 20 years, and they retain PSP longer than any other clams.

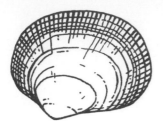

NATIVE LITTLENECK CLAM

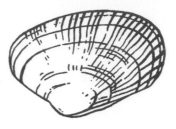

MANILA CLAM

HORSE (OR GAPER) CLAM

PURPLE VARNISH CLAM

BUTTER CLAM

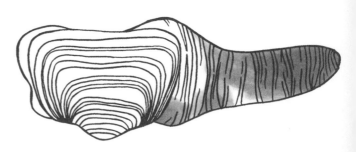

GEODUCK

Purple Varnish Clams

These clams have a thin mahogany-colored varnish on their shells. They are not native to the Salish Sea and were most likely introduced from Asia in discharged sea ballast from ships, but so far they are not considered invasive. They are among the smaller clams and rarely grow over 2.5 inches wide. They live in the upper third of the intertidal zone, 1 to 2 inches down in sand, mud, or gravel. Varnish clams are more freshwater tolerant than other clams and tend to congregate where there is freshwater runoff. They are considered edible, but be aware that their tolerance for freshwater also means they ingest pesticides, sewage effluence, and petroleum products from the freshwater runoff, which can collect in their flesh.

Geoducks

Geoducks (pronounced "gooey ducks") are the emperor of clams—the world's largest burrowing clam—huge and meaty, and a delicacy sought after by seafood cooks throughout the Pacific Northwest and Asia. "They taste like where we live," Naomi Tomky, food and drink writer, says, and I can think of no better way to describe their sea taste, sweetness, and umami. They grow to an average of 2 pounds with the shell expanding up to 10 inches wide. Geoducks are difficult to snag for the recreational digger and are available only in subtidal zones at extremely low tides (lower than minus 2 feet). Scoring a geoduck in the Northwest is a rite of passage and a great deal of work—but it is an iconic experience. Interested? Here is more information: bit.ly/2rZbPJa.

Dosewallips State Park is a good place to try when the tide is right; Duckabush State Park is as well.

Steamed Clams in Shallot Butter Sauce

MAKES 4 TO 6 SERVINGS

Steam these clams on a bonfire at the beach or make them at home. At the beach, you have license to toss the clamshells over your shoulder as you eat. Serve with a big loaf of crusty bread on the side to soak up the sauce. For open-fire cooking, you will need a camp grill, available at most sporting goods stores. Use it for all your beach-fire recipes.

INGREDIENTS:

½ cup salted butter

½ cup diced shallots

6 cloves garlic, chopped

2 cups sauvignon blanc or dry white wine of your choice

2 cups chopped fresh tomatoes, divided

1 bunch fresh flat-leaf parsley, stemmed and chopped, divided

Kosher salt and freshly ground black pepper

6 pounds manila or littleneck clams, scrubbed clean and purged if self-harvested

Build a campfire (see How to Build a Bonfire, page 60) and let it burn down to low flames and coals. Place a camp grill over the coals. Place a paella pan or other large, heavy-bottomed pan on the grill and add the butter. When the butter has melted, stir in the shallots and sauté for 2 minutes. Add the garlic and stir. Cook for 1 minute more. Add the wine, 1 cup of the tomatoes, and half of the chopped parsley. Season with salt and pepper, and add the clams. Using oven mitts, cover the pan tightly with aluminum foil. Steam the clams, shaking the pan frequently, for 5 to 6 minutes, or until the clams have opened. Remove the foil lid and, using tongs, discard any clams that remain closed. Add more salt and pepper to taste, sprinkle the remaining parsley and tomatoes over the steamed clams, and serve in bowls.

Beachside Clambake

MAKES 4 SERVINGS

These packets are easily put together and can be eaten straight out of the foil for easy, no-mess beach feasting. I like to serve them with crusty bread to dip into the sauce.

INGREDIENTS:

20 manila or littleneck clams, scrubbed clean and purged if self-harvested

2 ears fresh corn, cut into 2-inch rounds

1 cup thinly sliced green onions

4 plum tomatoes (about 8 ounces), chopped

1 large lemon, ends trimmed, and cut into 8 slices

4 cloves garlic, chopped

4 tablespoons chopped fresh basil

1 cup dry white wine

4 tablespoons salted butter

Kosher salt and freshly ground black pepper

4 tablespoons stemmed and chopped fresh Italian parsley

Build a campfire (see How to Build a Bonfire, page 60) and let it burn down to low flames and coals. Meanwhile, make the packets. Lay two 18-inch-long pieces of aluminum foil in a cross; make three other foil crosses for a total of four. Divide the clams, corn, onions, tomatoes, lemon, garlic, and basil evenly between the four foil packets in a single layer. Bring the sides of foil up and add ¼ cup of the wine and 1 tablespoon of the butter to each packet. Season with salt and pepper to taste.

Fold and roll the ends of the foil over, leaving a little headspace, and seal the packets securely closed. Lay the packets on the hot coals—make sure there are no flames or your packets can burn and leak. Cook for 20 to 25 minutes, or until the clams open. Carefully open the packets, discard any unopened clams, and sprinkle the parsley over the packets. Serve immediately.

SQUID

Squid jigging sounds like an Irish dance for mermaids, but don't let that mislead you. Jigging for squid is a fine way to spend a Northwest evening. Why do I love it so? It is the great egalitarian fishing activity on a public pier that uses inexpensive, uncomplicated gear and requires little experience. The public docks are a small United Nations of ethnic groups, and the camaraderie blooms as people share their tips and tricks beside you.

There are many types of squid, but you will be going for the Pacific squid called "opalescent," also known as "market squid." They grow up to 11 inches long and tend to travel in schools. When the catch is on, the dock will be a flurry of activity with young and old celebrating the imperceptible tug on the line and the reeling up of a gourmet meal.

Squid jigging is an inland-water activity with very little happening on the coasts. Public piers up and down Puget Sound are popular places to jig, with their bright lights attracting the schools to the piers. The squid begin to arrive late summer in the Strait of Juan de Fuca, and then move south and reach the Seattle/Tacoma area by October. Even though the squid fishery peaks in late November, begin on a late-summer night in Port Angeles and earn your chops, so you will be a squid-jigging master by Thanksgiving.

To follow squid-fishing catch results from fellow fishers, check out bit.ly/2qh2Ne9.

Where to Go

Washington

PORT ANGELES CITY PIER: The squid begin to arrive in late July through the Strait of Juan de Fuca, making **Port Angeles** one of the first places to try your luck. It is worth the ferry ride across the Sound if you are coming from the Seattle side and driving up the Olympic Peninsula. The best fishing is just after sunset; then the schools taper off and pick back up in the hours close to midnight. Make it a weekend getaway and spend the night at the sweet and utilitarian Downtown Hotel (PortAngelesDowntownHotel.com), a real bargain accommodation with bathrooms down the hall. It is a short walk to the public pier from there. The locals are enthusiastic and helpful on the dock, with seasoned squid veterans, parents, and kids mixing and mingling beside you. bit.ly/2s0r8RV

ODE TO PUBLIC PIERS

Open to the public and free, public piers are right up there with state parks and public libraries when it comes to making life bigger and better. This unique resource provides access to fishing grounds and bounty from the sea to those without boats or the money for a guide. The Puget Sound region has over sixty public piers from which to launch a kayak, drop a crab pot, jig for squid, or fish for salmon. Many are located along metro waterfronts and are accessible by public transportation. Public piers offer a year-round chance to catch a seafood dinner and a place where even the youngest can drop a line and experience the thrill of a wish turning into a fish.

For a list of all public fishing piers on Puget Sound, visit bit.ly/2r2eLaO.

EDMONDS FISHING PIER: This recently renovated pier just south of the ferry terminal in **Edmonds** is a hot spot for jiggers, with restrooms and rain shelters. It is well lit and attracts large schools of the baitfish that squid love. bit.ly/2r0HMSb

SEACREST BOATHOUSE AND PIER: You can catch a water taxi from downtown Seattle and land at the Seacrest pier in **West Seattle.** Two bonuses: some of the best views of the Seattle skyline, and boat rentals available adjacent to the pier if you decide to detour and spend time on the water. Seacrest is open 7 days a week and closes each night at 11:30 p.m. bit.ly/2r13SUE

ELLIOTT BAY PUBLIC FISHING PIER AT TERMINAL 86: Located in **Centennial Park** in **Seattle**, this large, 400-foot-long dock, complete with amenities—restrooms, rain shelters, and big lights down its length—has room for everyone. Walk through the park from the parking lot, or cross one of the two pedestrian bridges from Lower Queen Anne to access the pier. Fish On Bait and Tackle Shop (bit.ly/2u4gbAL) is at the entrance, and you can buy or rent your tackle and purchase a license here. Terminal 86 is one of the most popular public fishing piers in Puget Sound, and for good reason. bit.ly/2r25teX

LES DAVIS FISHING PIER: Located on **Commencement Bay** in **Tacoma**, this is another popular site for jigging. The pier is open 24 hours a day, 7 days a week with restrooms, rain shelters, and the strong overhead lights that attract squid. There are also picnic tables to enjoy an alfresco meal before dropping a line. bit.ly/2qkURV9

Equipment
- Shellfish license (see Resources, page 223)
- Inexpensive, lightweight pole (just about any spinning rod and reel will do)
- Squid jig: these weighted jigs have circles of hooks that look like bent pins and come in a variety of colors, but the fluorescent-green, hot-pink, and striped jigs work best
- Plastic bucket filled with a few inches of salt water
- Rain jacket and pants (particularly in fall and winter)
- Thermos (for a warm beverage)

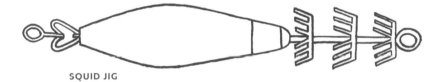

SQUID JIG

Technique

This is a nighttime fishery, and the key to success is knowing how deep the squid are, usually 10 to 20 feet down. Play with the depth of your line, starting shallow and then, if you have no luck, cast and drop the line a few feet deeper. Continue going down a few feet in depth with each cast until you hook one and then concentrate on that depth until the squid school moves on. After a cast, raise the rod to about 10 o'clock then lower it. Raise and lower the rod tip several times; the goal is to make the jig look like an injured fish that the squid will wrap its tentacles around, catching on the jig. There will be a tiny tug on the line when the squid hugs the jig, your signal to reel it in and drop it in the bucket. Try to keep slack out of the line or the squid will let go. There are no minimum size limits. The squid will keep in fresh seawater for several hours. Change the seawater if they "ink" into it.

How to Clean a Squid

- Grasp the squid tail in one hand and the head in the other. Pull with a slight twist. The head and viscera should slip apart.
- To remove the tentacles, cut just behind the eyes, then squeeze the cut tentacles to remove the beak (see Figure 1). Holding the mantle (body) with one hand, pinch the transparent spine (pen) with the other hand; pull it out and discard with the beak.
- Cut open the mantle lengthwise and scrape the viscera from the body with a knife or scissors (see Figure 2). Turn the mantle over and scrape the skin off the outer body.
- Rinse and blot the mantle dry. Place fresh squid on ice in a colander with a plate or bowl under it to catch the melt, cover them with a damp cloth, place in the refrigerator, and consume within 2 days. To freeze, place them in a heavy-duty freezer bag and remove all the air before sealing closed. Use within 2 months.

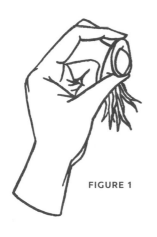

FIGURE 1

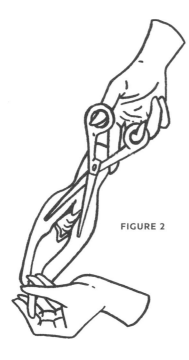

FIGURE 2

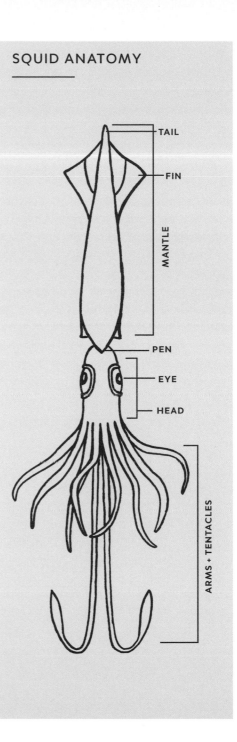

SQUID ANATOMY

TAIL

FIN

MANTLE

PEN

EYE

HEAD

ARMS + TENTACLES

Campfire Paella with Squid

MAKES 4 SERVINGS

A true paella is cooked over an open fire and eaten outdoors. Historically, field workers in Spain would cook a communal lunch in a heavy, flat pan laid on a fire. They threw in rice or beans, leftovers from dinner, and, if they were lucky, some seafood or rabbit. The wood smoke from the fire and the spices pulled from the land added a unique and complex flavor, and paella evolved to a national dish. For open-fire cooking, you will need a camp grill, available at most sporting goods stores. Eat from the pan with your fellow campers and top off the meal with a cold bottle of Spanish Rioja wine.

FOR THE SQUID:

1 pound whole squid tentacles and ½-inch-thick rounds

1 tablespoon olive oil

1 clove garlic, minced

¼ teaspoon smoked hot paprika

¼ teaspoon salt

FOR THE PAELLA:

4 skinless, boneless chicken thighs, cut into small pieces

1½ teaspoons kosher salt, divided

½ teaspoon cracked black pepper

2 tablespoons olive oil

7 cloves garlic, minced

1 medium Spanish onion (about 8 ounces), diced

1 red bell pepper (about 8 ounces), cut into strips

4 plum tomatoes (about 8 ounces), chopped

1 teaspoon freshly ground black pepper

2 cups Arborio or Bomba rice

3 cups chicken broth

1 cup dry white wine

4 saffron threads

2 teaspoons smoked hot paprika

1 (8-ounce) cured chorizo, cut into rounds

Lemon wedges, for serving

Build a campfire (see How to Build a Bonfire, page 60) and let it burn down to low flames and coals. To prepare the squid, in a medium bowl, toss the tentacles and slices with the oil, garlic, paprika, and salt. Set aside.

CONTINUED

In a small bowl, toss the chicken thigh pieces with ½ teaspoon of the salt and the cracked black pepper.

Place the camp grill over the coals, and place a paella or roasting pan on the grill. Add the olive oil, swirl it around, and then add the chicken. Cook, turning occasionally, for 5 to 6 minutes, or until the chicken is still a bit underdone, then push the pieces to the outer edges of the pan. Add the garlic, onion, bell pepper, tomatoes, remaining 1 teaspoon salt, and ground black pepper to the pan. Sauté, stirring, for 5 to 8 minutes, or until the vegetables begin to brown. Add the rice, stir to combine, and sauté for 1 to 2 minutes. Add the broth, wine, saffron, and paprika, and bring to a simmer. Place the squid evenly over the rice mixture, and add the chorizo. Rotate the pan and stir occasionally until all the liquid is absorbed, about 30 minutes or more, depending on the heat of your fire. Spread the coals to the side if necessary to avoid burning the rice. You are aiming for *socarrat*, a beautiful word for rice that gets a little crunchy at the bottom of the pan; the rice should smell toasted and almost make a crackling sound. When done, remove the pan from the fire, cover with aluminum foil, and let stand for 10 minutes. Serve with lemon wedges.

NOTE: To make it easier at camp, prepare the meat, seafood, and vegetables beforehand, place in separate ziplock bags, and store in a cooler until needed.

TIPS AND TRICKS FOR COOKING ON AN OPEN FIRE

- Cook with the coals, not the flames. Get the fire going at least an hour before you start cooking for a more consistent heat, and push more coals underneath the pan as they burn down.
- Use fire pits at campgrounds when available.
- Your pots and pans will blacken with soot, so browse thrift shops for heavy pans to use for campfire cooking only.
- Invest in an inexpensive fire grill with legs that you can set over the coals. This helps to keep the pan level.
- Keep in mind that cooking over an open fire may take more time than cooking on your stovetop at home.
- Always extinguish the fire at the end of the night.

BLACKBERRIES

The Pacific Northwest is stitched with blackberry vines sprawling and spilling from vacant lots, roadsides, and coastal shores. Himalayan blackberries, or *Rubus procerus*, are everywhere. They were introduced by Luther Burbank in 1885, who exchanged seeds with a source in India; those few seedlings ran wild from California to deep into British Columbia. Today they are considered an invasive plant nearly impossible to eradicate. You have to hire a herd of goats to keep them in check, but there is a silver lining to the wall of thorns in late summer, and that is the berry.

Although Himalayan blackberries are the most common, the native Pacific trailing blackberry (*Rubus ursinus*) produces a more rare and delicious berry with fewer seeds and a more intense flavor. They grow on slender, trailing vines that hug the ground on sunny coastal slopes, but these treasures can be hard to find. They are very expensive in stores if you can find them.

If you are not a gourmand and want an easy-to-find-and-pick bucket of berries, go Himalayan.

Tips and Techniques
- To avoid crushing the berries, use a shallow container for picking.
- The fruit should be shiny and firm and come off the stem easily.
- Avoid picking beside busy roads (there will be too much car exhaust and pollutants on the fruit)—and avoid berries low to the ground, where dogs leave their messages.
- To reach the inner sanctum of a blackberry barricade, drop a wide board into the shrubbery.
- Do not wash the berries until just before you are ready to use them.
- To freeze extra berries, lightly rinse them in a colander, shake out the excess water, place the berries in a single layer on a baking sheet covered with parchment, and freeze for several hours. Place the frozen berries in a ziplock bag.
- To get rid of blackberry stains on clothes, stretch the fabric over a big bowl and carefully pour boiling water over it. Next soak the item in white vinegar for 30 minutes. Rinse out the vinegar and wash as usual.

Blackberry Basil Mojito

MAKES 1 COCKTAIL

To take this drink to the beach, mix everything but the club soda together and place it in a thermos. Add the club soda when you are ready to imbibe. You can substitute rum or tequila for the vodka if desired.

INGREDIENTS:

4 fresh basil leaves, plus more for garnish

4 ripe blackberries, plus more for garnish

2 teaspoons Ginger-Infused Simple Syrup (recipe follows)

2 ounces vodka

Ice cubes

Club soda

In a small bowl, gently muddle the basil, blackberries, and syrup. Stir in the vodka, and strain into a glass filled with ice. Top off with club soda, stir, and garnish with a basil leaf and a blackberry.

Ginger-Infused Simple Syrup

MAKES ABOUT 2 CUPS

Use leftover ginger-infused simple syrup in other summer cocktails. It will keep in the refrigerator for up to a month.

INGREDIENTS:
1 cup granulated sugar
1 cup water

1 (4-inch) finger fresh
  ginger, cut into thin
  rounds (no need to peel)

In a medium saucepan over high heat, combine the sugar, water, and ginger, and bring to a boil. Reduce the heat to medium low, and simmer for 10 minutes. Remove from the heat, and set aside to cool. When cool, strain into a jar, seal, and place in the refrigerator.

Beach Projects

BEACH VOLCANO

Kids can do this fun project on a beach multiple times without adults worrying about another mess to clean up afterward. The measurements are forgiving; just add more vinegar and baking soda after the first flow for more action.

WHAT YOU WILL NEED:
Small trowel
1 (16.9-ounce) plastic
  water bottle
1 teaspoon liquid
  dish soap
3 tablespoons
  baking soda
1 funnel
¼ cup water
Several drops red
  food coloring
½ cup white or apple
  cider vinegar

Use the trowel to dig several inches down in the sand; set the bottle in the hole, then build a mountain shape of damp sand around it, leaving the opening clear. Add the dish soap and baking soda to the bottle using the funnel. Add the water and food coloring, then pour in the vinegar and watch the lava stream and spill. The baking soda and vinegar react to produce carbon dioxide and create the "lava" that pours out just like in real volcanoes.

SAND CANDLES

I first did this project many years ago with our four young children on an island in British Columbia. The men were out fishing for king salmon in Barkley Sound; the kids and I wandered to the beach, swinging cans and buckets, to build sand castles. It was sunny, the island was green and dreamy, and we had all the time in the world to spend: we were rich. You can purchase cotton string and candlewicks at candle-making and general craft supply stores.

FOR THE FIRE:
Driftwood
Matches
Newspaper or
   fire starter

FOR THE CANDLE:
Small trowel
1 (1-pound) box paraffin

1 large metal can
Wax crayons (optional)
Scissors or sharp
   pocketknife
Cotton string or
   candlewicks
1 pencil-thin stick
Pot holder

WICK SETUP

To build the fire, using the trowel, dig a shallow depression in the sand and place rocks around the depression to contain it. Build a small fire (see How to Build a Bonfire, page 60). To make the candle, place the paraffin in the metal can, add the crayon for color, and set it on the flames. While waiting for the wax to melt, dig a small hole in the sand with a flattened bottom about the size of your fist. Cut a piece of string to match the depth of the hole, with enough left over to tie around the middle of the thin stick. Rest the stick over the hole, use the pot holder to grab the metal can, and pour in the melted wax. The wax will cool and harden in approximately an hour depending on the temperature of the sand. Lift the candle from the sand and brush off the excess. A nice shell of sand will remain around your candle. Be sure to burn this candle on a plate or in a jar that can get messy!

COLLECTED STARDUST

It's dusty out there in our solar system. Every day up to 100 tons of cosmic dust fall to earth, mostly micrometeorite particles that have collided with our planet every day since its beginning, leaving a surprising amount of debris. It is possible to collect a few of these meteor particles because they are composed of nickel and iron, substances attracted to a magnet, and a sandy beach is one of the best places to find them. You can find magnets at any hardware store.

WHAT YOU WILL NEED:

Strong magnet

Sandwich-size plastic bag

Magnifying glass

Place the magnet in the plastic bag and drag it through dry sand at the beach. You will collect an amazing amount of what looks like black salt. Turn the bag inside out and rub the bits from the magnet back into the bag. Look at the bits under the magnifying glass. Around 20 percent of these pieces are tiny micrometeorites: stardust in your hand.

KIDS' DAY AT THE BEACH ADVENTURE ESSENTIALS

- Waterproof sunscreen
- Sunglasses and hats
- First-aid kit with Band-Aids, antibiotic ointment, and tweezers for splinters
- Instant cold pack for bumps and bruises
- Extra clothes
- Picnic lunch
- Snacks
- Beach towels
- Water bottles
- Beach blanket
- Wet wipes
- Old kitchen utensils and small trowels, for digging
- Ball of twine, for tying together things like sticks for a shelter
- Pocketknife
- Plastic bags, for collections, garbage, and wet clothes
- Sand toys
- Small bottle of bubbles, for when all else fails

BEACHSIDE SHADE

Some of the best moments of summer are spent sprawled on a blanket on the beach with big pillows, a good book, and a nap. When the sun is hot, you need shade. Luckily, most beaches in the Pacific Northwest have the ingredients for a winsome canopy made with a few things from home and driftwood and rocks from the beach. If you have to buy the canopy fabric, you will reuse it over and over. It helps to have two people for the construction of the shade, but it's possible to do this on your own.

WHAT YOU WILL NEED:

7 (6- to 8-foot-long) driftwood sticks, about as thick as your wrist

Ball of sturdy twine

Sharp pocketknife

Lightweight cotton batik bedspread, or 10 feet sheer lightweight fabric

Big rocks, for weighing down the fabric

Start by making a tripod with three of the sticks by holding the sticks together and, about a foot down from the top, weaving the twine tightly in and around them, going over and under several times until you have wrapped them securely together. Use the knife to cut the twine (and to cut cheese and apples and salami for a snack afterward). Make another tripod with the other three sticks in the same manner. Spread one tripod out and stand it upright in the sand. Set the other tripod in the sand less than the bedspread length away. Lay the last stick across the top of the tripods, and you have a frame for the fabric. Tie one end of the fabric to each tripod, allowing the other two ends to dangle in the sand, then pull the fabric out slightly and lay big rocks on the edges to hold it out. Add pillows and a blanket inside, and indulge in the fine art of napping.

On the Water

PADDLEBOARDING

Stand-up paddleboarding (SUP) is the fastest-growing water sport in the world. It's easy to see why: you are outdoors and upright on the water with a grand view of what is below you, and it is an excellent full-body workout far from the confines of the gym. If you get hooked, most places that rent SUPs sell them at the end of the season at a discount. Once you're familiar with the basics, consider trying paddleboard yoga; lessons are available at many of the rental locations mentioned below.

Where to Rent SUPs

British Columbia
- **VANCOUVER:** Wazsup (Wazsup.ca), Ecomarine Paddlesport Centre (Ecomarine.com), Vancouver Water Adventures (VancouverWaterAdventures.com)
- **TOFINO:** T'ashii Paddle School (bit.ly/2qheAZP)
- **SALT SPRING ISLAND:** Salt Spring Adventure Company (bit.ly/2qNSmPs)
- **VICTORIA:** Ocean River Sports (OceanRiver.com)

Washington
- **SEATTLE:** Washington Surf Academy (bit.ly/2ijqICS), POPsup (bit.ly/2qM3sR3), Northwest Paddle Surfers Lake Washington (NorthwestPaddleSurfers.com)
- **VASHON ISLAND:** Fat Cat Paddleboarding (bit.ly/2rRsJh2)
- **TACOMA:** Dolan's Board Sports (DolansBoardSports.com), Foss Harbor Marina (FossHarborMarina.com)

MICRO-ADVENTURE: SURF A SHIP'S WAKE

Surf a ship's wake wave on Puget Sound using your stand-up paddle-board. After the ships have passed, freighter waves break like regular old surf waves, perfect for beginners. Salmon Bay Paddle (SalmonBayPaddle .com) offers classes in **Ballard** for this crazy-fun adventure. If you want to try it on your own, check out this cool live website that shows all vessel traffic and each ship's gross tonnage: bit.ly/2rVVk1l.

Oregon
- **ASTORIA:** Clatsop Paddle Company (ClatsopPaddle.com)
- **MANZANITA:** SUP Manzanita (SUPManzanita.com)

Equipment
- Stand-up paddleboard: Beginners should choose a stable board that is 30 inches wide and at least 11 feet long
- SUP paddle
- Personal flotation device
- Ankle leash, to keep the board from drifting away if you fall
- Sunglasses and sunscreen

Technique

TO STAND: Make it easy on yourself and start in calm, flat water. Float the SUP into the water until the fin no longer touches the bottom. First kneel just behind the center of the board, then stand, one foot at a time. Place your feet side by side, hip-distance apart, in the center of the board. Don't look down; keep your eyes on the horizon. Bend your knees slightly and balance from the hips.

TO PADDLE: Hold the paddle with the curved angle of the blade away from you. It's counterintuitive and a common beginner mistake to hold it with the curve toward you. Next, place one hand on the top grip of the paddle and the other down the shaft, shoulder-width apart from the top hand.

TO STROKE: Keep your arms straight with a slight bend at the elbows. Reach the paddle forward and fully submerge the blade in the water. Pull the paddle toward you using your back and abdominal muscles. Think of the torso as your engine, not your arms. End the stroke when the paddle is even with your feet. Hint: Start out with short, slow strokes, build a rhythm, and keep the paddle close to the board on your stroke to propel yourself in a straighter line, as opposed to paddling angled out wide from the board.

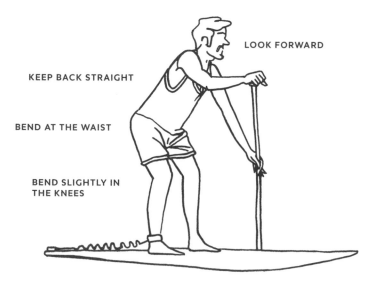

LOOK FORWARD

KEEP BACK STRAIGHT

BEND AT THE WAIST

BEND SLIGHTLY IN
THE KNEES

FULL-MOON KAYAK PADDLE

It's a full moon. Paddling across the sea at night with only the light of the moon to guide you is magical. The companies listed below have all you need to make it happen.

British Columbia
- VANCOUVER: Ecomarine Paddlesport Centre (Ecomarine.com)
- VICTORIA: Victoria Waterfront Tours (bit.ly/2qp3ddL)
- SOOKE: Kayak Rush Adventures (Rush-Adventures.com)

Washington
- BELLINGHAM: Community Boating Center (BoatingCenter.org)
- ORCAS ISLAND: Shearwater Kayak Tours (ShearwaterKayaks.com)
- WHIDBEY ISLAND: Whidbey Island Kayaking (WhidbeyIslandKayaking.com)
- SEATTLE: Alki Kayak Tours and Adventure Center (bit.ly/2s5rXfO)
- VASHON ISLAND: Vashon Watersports (VashonWatersports.com)

Oregon
- TILLAMOOK: Kayak Tillamook (KayakTillamook.com)

MICRO-ADVENTURE: SKIMBOARDING

Skimboarding may have its roots in boredom. In the 1920s lifeguards in Laguna Beach, California, came up with a flat, round board they threw along the water's edge to hydroplane through the shallow water. This caught the attention of beach visitors who went home and made their own. Today's skimboards are more surfboard shaped for greater control, and they are lighter than the originals. Skimboarding is tricky and combines the skill sets of surfing and snowboarding as you toss the board in a few inches of water along the shoreline. You will fly. You will fall. You will have fun. Check your local surf shop for skimboard rentals and more information. For inspiration, watch the DB Pro/AM skimboard competition in July at Dash Point State Park in Federal Way, Washington. DBSkimboards.com

BIOLUMINESCENCE TOURS

The first time you encounter bioluminescence in the sea, you do not forget it. It is the aurora borealis of water, a dreamy, otherworldly glow that outlines moving bodies in salt water—from schools of fish to humans to rocks thrown off a dock. I live on a bay rich in the dinoflagellates called *Noctiluca scintillans*, a plankton that emits a blue-green radiance when disturbed. We have a summer tradition of firing up the steam hut to sweat and then jumping off the dock into the cold Sound, where the movement of our bodies agitates the single-cell organisms into throwing off an incandescent light. Our waving arms and legs leave trails of sparkles as we watch glowing schools of fish moving beside us, until a seal gliding by in a nuclear blaze sends us propelling to shore.

A dark summer night is the best time for viewing bioluminescence. The warmer water of the season encourages the dinoflagellate plankton bloom that emits light when disturbed. Bioluminescence is rarer in Oregon, but you can make the sands glow by scuffing your feet along the sandy shore of a beach after a bloom. Watch the local press in Oregon beachside towns; they often report the locations of the blooms when they occur. To experience these star shots in the water, take a tour with one of the operators listed here, or contact your local kayak company and ask if they will arrange one. Many will do custom bioluminescence tours even if it is not listed on their website.

Washington
- BELLINGHAM: Community Boating Center (BoatingCenter.org)
- SAN JUAN ISLAND: Discovery Sea Kayaks (bit.ly/2r1qFiU)
- WHIDBEY ISLAND: Whidbey Island Kayaking (offers custom bioluminescence tours; WhidbeyIslandKayaking.com)
- KINGSTON: Kingston Adventures (KingstonAdventures.com)
- VASHON ISLAND: Vashon Watersports (VashonWatersports.com)

On Your Own

Choose a windless night with no moon. Ambient light from buildings and docks can also dim the effect. Find a quiet cove on Puget Sound and splash your feet in the water or, even better, take the plunge and swim. Good places around the Sound are Liberty Bay in **Poulsbo**, Hidden Cove Park on **Bainbridge Island**, and Quartermaster Harbor on **Vashon Island**.

CITIZEN SCIENCE: MONITOR HIGH-RISK WASHINGTON BEACHES FOR BACTERIA

Beach Environment Assessment, Communication, and Health (BEACH) is a program that asks volunteers to take samples from high-risk beaches to test for an indicator bacteria called *enterococci*. High-risk beaches are those popular with recreational users and located near bacteria sources such as failing septic tanks from beachfront homes, sewage treatment plants, where boating is popular, or where animal waste (from cattle, for example) can leach into the water. The presence of *enterococci* means there is a greater potential for disease-causing bacteria and viruses in the water that can impact humans. Volunteers collect three samples at knee depth using sterile techniques taught by BEACH, and the samples are then delivered to a lab for analysis. Understanding the risks to people from polluted water offers a chance to also understand what we can do to reduce the risk. For more information on how you can help, visit bit.ly/2qhzND0.

Celebrations & Nature

PERSEID METEOR SHOWER

The summer night sky's most spectacular show is the Perseid meteor shower, which peaks between August 10 and 12 as Earth moves through the dust and debris trail of Comet Swift-Tuttle. It is a dazzling display our family watched for years from an old trampoline in the backyard. We spread out blankets and pillows and turned our eyes to the heavens, our busy lives pausing while the vault of shooting stars created a night to remember. They are easy to spot; all you need are clear skies and your eyes. Look up. There are shooting stars out there.

Tips and Tricks
- Go outside under a wide sky and away from city lights if possible. If the moon is out, it can affect viewing, but the brighter meteors will still be visible.
- Allow 30 minutes for your eyes to adjust to the dark.
- Lie flat on your back on a blanket or look into the northeastern section of the sky, where the meteors originate from.
- Prepare to wait and bring snacks and beverages.
- Stay awake! The best time of night to see the most meteors is from after midnight until just before dawn.
- The Perseids are known for their colors and have more fireballs, or ultrabright meteors, than any other shower.
- Meteors can come from all directions, but they always travel from the constellation they are named after, in this case Perseus in the northeastern section of the sky.

Astronomical associations and societies are excellent resources to learn more about our night skies. They have events and classes that will introduce you to galaxies and constellations, with many of the associations owning telescopes that can peer deep into the universe.

British Columbia
- VANCOUVER: Royal Astronomical Society of Vancouver (RASC-Vancouver .com)
- VICTORIA: Royal Astronomical Society of Canada (Victoria.RASC.ca)

Washington
- BAINBRIDGE ISLAND: Battle Point Astronomical Association (BPAstro.org)
- SEATTLE: Seattle Astronomical Society (SeattleAstro.org)
- TACOMA: Tacoma Astronomical Society (TAS-Online.org)

Oregon
- PORTLAND: Rose City Astronomers (RoseCityAstronomers.net)

SUMMER SOLSTICE BONFIRE

The longest day of the year in the northern hemisphere is either June 20 or 21—technically the summer solstice is the instant the sun is directly overhead the Tropic of Cancer. It is a tradition the world over to celebrate this day filled with light. Weddings are planned, bonfires burn, and crowds do sun salutations in Times Square. There is science to back up our festive moods. In 2011 researchers began analyzing the random tweets of several million people in many nations for two years and found that with the days of increasing light, people expressed more buoyant moods, and the reverse happened as winter solstice approached. On the summer solstice, we are happier people.

In ancient days in Finland, big bonfires were ignited at the summer solstice to keep evil spirits at bay. To encourage good fortune, tradition held that the people must get drunk and raucous beside the fire to invite abundant crops and good luck. Whatever your abundant crop and good luck is, choose this night for revelry with a bonfire on the beach. Invite your friends, bring a feast, and light the fire.

Tips and Tricks

- Check for burn bans before lighting your fire. Go here for the Puget Sound region: bit.ly/2xZnuiF. For Oregon State Parks call the information line at 800-551-6949. In British Columbia: bit.ly/2s0iXp5.
- Bring plenty of blankets to lounge on.
- If you start the revelry in the afternoon, make a beach shade (see page 49).
- Bring finger foods for the picnic to reduce the need for hauling cutlery and dishes. Serve the food on wooden cutting boards with serving utensils.
- Don't forget wet wipes for after eating s'mores.
- Stay hydrated and refreshed! Freeze half-filled water bottles, then fill the rest of the way with tap water.
- Pour water on the fire and cover it with sand at the end of the evening to extinguish it.

Menu Ideas

- Wild smoked salmon appetizers: Spread a thin layer of cream cheese on a triangle of dark pumpernickel bread. Place a chunk of smoked salmon on top. Arrange the appetizers on a platter, then scatter rings of red onion and a sprinkling of capers over them all.
- A loaf of crusty bread with prosciutto, salami, chorizo, or other thin-sliced hams or sausages, and a variety of cheeses.
- Caprese skewers: On wooden skewers, line up small balls of mozzarella interspersed with cherry tomatoes and basil.
- Grapes, strawberries, sliced apples.
- Hummus served with triangle toasts of pita bread.
- Marinated olives.
- Gourmet salted caramel s'mores: Toast a marshmallow, place it on a graham cracker, drizzle your favorite caramel sauce over the marshmallow, sprinkle a little sea salt over it all, and top with another graham cracker.

HOW TO BUILD A BONFIRE

What you will need:
- Cotton balls
- Petroleum jelly
- Plastic bag
- Newspaper
- Kindling and logs from home, or use driftwood from the beach if it is allowed (research ahead of time)
- Matches or a lighter
- Bucket
- Small shovel

Before you leave home, make a DIY no-fail fire starter: cover the cotton balls with petroleum jelly, and place them in a plastic bag (note: don't burn plastic bag; discard after use). At the beach, scrape a shallow hole in the sand—the bigger the fire, the bigger the hole. This also helps to shield the first flames from wind. Next place crumpled newspaper and several balls of fire starter (pulled apart slightly) in the center of the hole, then cross small, dry pieces of kindling on top.

- Light the fire and add plenty of small- to medium-size dry sticks as it burns.
- Add bigger pieces of wood, teepee style.
- As the fire burns, continue adding driftwood or logs until the fire is your desired size.
- When finished with the fire, pour water on the fire and bury the coals with sand using the small shovel.

Festivals & Events

SAND CASTLE COMPETITIONS

Sand castle art takes two ingredients: sand and water, simple materials for creating magnificent sculptures that are swept away by the tide.

British Columbia

Parksville | *Parksville Beach Festival*
This monthlong, world-class event is held from mid-July to mid-August on an expansive and gorgeous sandy beach on **Vancouver Island**. The judging is within the first few days, with public viewing from 9:00 a.m. to 9:00 p.m. daily throughout the month. There are many activities and events scheduled, including fireworks, free sculpting lessons and demos, and a festival for kids. ParksvilleBeachFest.ca

Washington

Edmonds | *Sand Castle Contest*
This entertaining and very relaxed contest is usually held in late July or mid-August at the fabulous Edmonds Marina Beach Park. It is free and perfect for budding sand engineers who want to get their hands dirty making art. You can work on your own or form a team for a 2-hour shot at creating a masterpiece. Open to all ages. bit.ly/2qkcqJi

Ocean Shores | *The Sand and Sawdust Festival*
This festival is held at the end of June and showcases both sand sculpting and chainsaw art—a real Northwest combination! The sand sculpture contest has a family division as well as a professional division, and there are lessons and workshops on technique offered. Take home a party favor: the wood carvings are auctioned off at the end of each day. It's a big festival that draws over forty thousand people; make your lodging reservations early. bit.ly/2qSsltA

Long Beach | The Sandsations
This 4-day festival in mid-July has the main competition on Saturday, when artists are given 6 hours—from 6:00 a.m. to noon—to begin and complete their creations. Sandsations also has a bonfire, a boardwalk dance, and free s'mores. SandsationsLongBeach.com

Oregon

Cannon Beach | The Sandcastle Contest
One of the oldest sand castle competitions in the United States, this mid-June **Cannon Beach** event features not only elaborate sand sculpting but a bonfire on the beach and a 5K fun run on Sunday. It's a popular event. Make your campsite or hotel reservation early. bit.ly/2s4CFiW

OUTDOOR MUSIC BY THE SHORE

Take a summer night, sprawl on a blanket outdoors, add music, and you have all you need for an enchanting evening. There are outdoor concerts staged in communities up and down the Pacific Northwest coast; check out your local events calendar for more listings.

British Columbia

Bamfield | Music by the Sea
Music by the Sea is an extraordinary experience. Set in a beautiful inlet on the remote west coast of **Vancouver Island**, this 9-day series of concerts includes chamber music, opera, and jazz performed by eminent musicians from all over the world. Christopher Donison, founder and executive artistic director of Music by the Sea, believes the remote location helps musicians "to focus the muse." It must be true; the music is transcendent. Accommodation is limited and many people bring their boats to anchor in the bay for the series. MusicbytheSea.ca

Vancouver
It's a city of music with a wide range of free concerts over the summer. Here are a few festivals not to miss:

CARNAVAL DEL SOL: This Latin-themed carnival is held on the second weekend in July and features live bands from Latin America. CarnavaldelSol.ca

TD VANCOUVER INTERNATIONAL JAZZ FESTIVAL: There are free and ticketed concerts in this series throughout the Vancouver metro area from late June until the first weekend in July. bit.ly/2qM0DQ9

MUSICAL NOONERS: Enjoy free concerts at noon every weekday outside the Canadian Broadcasting Corporation building on Hamilton Street. It runs from the second week in July to mid-August. bit.ly/2ssruR9

SUMMER SESSIONS CONCERTS: Shipbuilders' Square in North Vancouver is the setting for these concerts on Saturday nights from early July to the end of August. bit.ly/2qX5SyF

Washington

Friday Harbor | Music in the Park
Bring a picnic and enjoy the free summer concert series on Friday evenings from 5:00 to 7:00 p.m. and on Sunday afternoons from 2:00 to 4:00 p.m., held from the first Friday in July to September 1 at the Port of Friday Harbor on **San Juan Island.** bit.ly/2h0p3FG

Port Townsend | The Festival of American Fiddle Tunes
The festival is a weeklong workshop for fiddlers from all over the world held at Fort Worden State Park. Workshop teachers and participants offer three public concerts during the week—a great opportunity to listen to some fine toe-tapping bluegrass and explore the charms of Port Townsend. bit.ly/2qXe8il

Woodinville | Summer Concert Series at Chateau Ste. Michelle Winery
The series offers concerts that range from blues to rock and jazz, and performers include musical masters like Paul Simon, Diana Krall, and Lyle Lovett. Tickets go fast for the more popular concerts; watch for a press

release from the winery in March for the schedule. Concerts are held from the end of May to mid-September. bit.ly/2s4DHMd

Seattle
CONCERTS AT THE MURAL: Sponsors KEXP (Seattle's independent alternative/indie rock station) and the Seattle Center roll out a diverse lineup of musical artists for this series. The concerts are staged at the Mural Amphitheater at the Seattle Center Friday evenings for the month of August; they are for all ages, free, and musically free ranging, like listening to KEXP live. bit.ly/1rYRXkt

OUT TO LUNCH CONCERT SERIES: Add live music to your lunch with this very popular series held at City Hall Plaza and various other downtown locations from the beginning of July through the month of August every day of the week, from 12:00 to 1:30 p.m. bit.ly/2rHEWV4

SUMMER CONCERTS AT THE LOCKS: Listen to free music in a unique setting, the Ballard Locks, where boats and salmon can travel between freshwater and Puget Sound. The series is held late May through September on most Saturdays and Sundays, with the music ranging from jazz to blues to big band. bit.ly/2lycR0m

Tacoma | Jazz Under the Stars
This is a fabulous series of professional jazz concerts sponsored by Pacific Lutheran University, free to the public and with side benefits: free coffee, wine and snacks available to buy, and sometimes star gazing after the concert at PLU's W. M. Keck Observatory. In bad weather the concerts are held in Lagerquist Concert Hall on campus. bit.ly/1eeEwKT

Ilwaco | Waikiki Concert Series
The concerts take place on Waikiki Beach, a small pocket beach at Cape Disappointment State Park. Check out the Maya Lin Confluence Project, a series of art installations commemorating the Lewis and Clark expedition, while you are there. The Pacific Ocean is the backdrop for music that plays like a cinematic score to the evening. The concerts are held on the second and fourth Saturdays in June, July, and August from 7:00 to 8:30 p.m. A Washington State Discover Pass is required to attend. bit.ly/2zlQZLU

Oregon

Astoria | Astoria Music Festival
Every June this festival produces nearly 3 weeks of world-class opera, classical, and chamber music. Do you love opera? Their operatic productions have been cited by the *Oregonian* as one of the "Top Ten Classical Music Performances in the Pacific Northwest." AstoriaMusicFestival.org

Manzanita | Manzanita Music Festival
This 3-day family-friendly concert series highlights a variety of genres by local, regional, and national artists in July. ManzanitaMusicFestival.org

Lincoln City | Siletz Bay Music Festival
Enjoy two weeks of concerts in classical, jazz, and musical theater performances. The festival runs from late June to early July. SiletzBayMusic.org

MICRO-ADVENTURE: NIGHT BIKE RIDE

Ride in a sponsored night bike ride with city lights and bikes glowing down urban streets. Most major metropolitan areas have summer night rides. Here are a few to pique your interest:
- Vancouver, British Columbia: HUB Bike the Night (BikeHub.ca /BiketheNight)
- Seattle, Washington: Cascade Bicycle Club (Cascade.org)
- Portland, Oregon: Thursday Night Ride (bit.ly/2hsyhaC)

AUTUMN

Outings

MULTIDAY BIKE TRIPS

5-Day Cycling Trip in the Gulf Islands | *5 days*

Autumn is the perfect time for multiday cycling trips in the Pacific Northwest. The crowds are gone, traffic is down, and the weather is divine. The following 5-day exploration of several **Southern Gulf Islands** is gorgeous but can be physically demanding. Be prepared for detours and rest stops, and plan to stay in resorts and inns by night. When planning your trip, check out the current ferry schedule to the Southern Gulf Islands (bit.ly/2r6BNxe) to coordinate your trip to each island.

Begin in **Victoria** and cycle 18 miles on the scenic Lochside Regional Trail (bit.ly/2qrT6oE), a former railway line, to the **Swartz Bay** ferry terminal in **Sidney**. Other than some of the steeper climbs on the islands, finding the start of the Lochside Regional Trail was the hardest part of this dreamy trip. Once on the Lochside Regional Trail, approximately 7 miles north of Victoria, stop for lunch at Mattick's Farm (MatticksFarm.com), a collection of shops and restaurants in **Cordova Bay**. There is also a good liquor store here, Liquor Plus, to stock up on wine and spirits. The ride from Victoria to Swartz Bay will take approximately 2 hours (not including a lunch stop). Continue on from Mattick's Farm to Swartz Bay for the BC Ferry to **Galiano Island**. When you reach the ferry, you will dismount and walk onboard. After the likely early morning rising and 18 miles of riding, you will be happy to call it a day at Galiano Oceanfront Inn and Spa (GalianoInn.com), right next to the ferry landing. Spend two nights here to give yourself time to explore the island. Biking on the Southern Gulf Islands can be hilly with precipitous inclines, and you will encounter even athletic cyclists walking their bikes up some of the steeps, but the light traffic, views, and laid-back charm make it all worth it.

The next day stash your bike in the bushes and hike 2 miles up Mount Galiano for spectacular views. Have lunch and a brew at the Hummingbird Pub (HummingbirdPub.com) in **Sturdies Bay**, or cycle back to the inn for a steam and a massage. Another possibility for the day: rent a boat from Galiano Moped and Boat Rental (GalianoAdventures.com) in **Montague Harbour** and go salmon fishing, or check out the beaches and bays of the island from the water.

The next stop is **Saturna Island**, one of the least visited islands with only 350 residents and miles of empty road along the Strait of Georgia. The ferry service to Saturna Island is generally limited; only Saturdays and Sundays have morning ferries from Galiano Island. The rest of the week ferries leave and arrive at night, so check the schedule and plan well. When you arrive, spend the day biking East Point Road, where there are numerous access points to remote beaches along the Strait of Georgia. Check out the East Point Lighthouse on the easternmost point of the island. It is considered the Gulf Islands' best site for land-based whale watching, with sightings common May through November. Cycle back to Saturna Lodge (Saturna.ca), just over a mile from the ferry, to spend the night. Your ferry leaves the next morning for Pender Island.

If you arrive on **Pender Island** on a Saturday, you're in luck—the farmers' market is held on Bedwell Harbour Road, on the way to Poet's Cove Resort (PoetsCove.com), your accommodation for the next 2 nights. This is a classic autumn market with a bounty of vegetables and fruits, homemade baked goods, artisan crafts and jams, and a mouthwatering variety of lunch and picnic provisions. After browsing the market, detour north to check out the sweet and funky community of **Hope Bay**, then proceed south down Bedwell Harbour Road to South Pender Island and the Poet's Cove Resort on Spaulding Road.

Poet's Cove Resort is an ideal place to reward your weary self after biking all the hills to get there. There is a fine spa on site with a eucalyptus steam cave and hot tub, massages, and manicures. Brooks Point Park is a short bike ride or walk from Poet's Cove and has a sheltered beach; a large, grassy meadow; and breathtaking views of the sea. During your stay consider an afternoon's cycle to Sea Star Estate Farm and Winery (SeastarVineyards.ca), where they produce award-winning wines, or there is always the lure of the salmon to pull you from the bike and onto the sea. Saltwater Moon Fishing and Boat Charter (GulfIslandsFishing.com) will meet you right there at the marina at Poet's Cove Resort and take you out for the day.

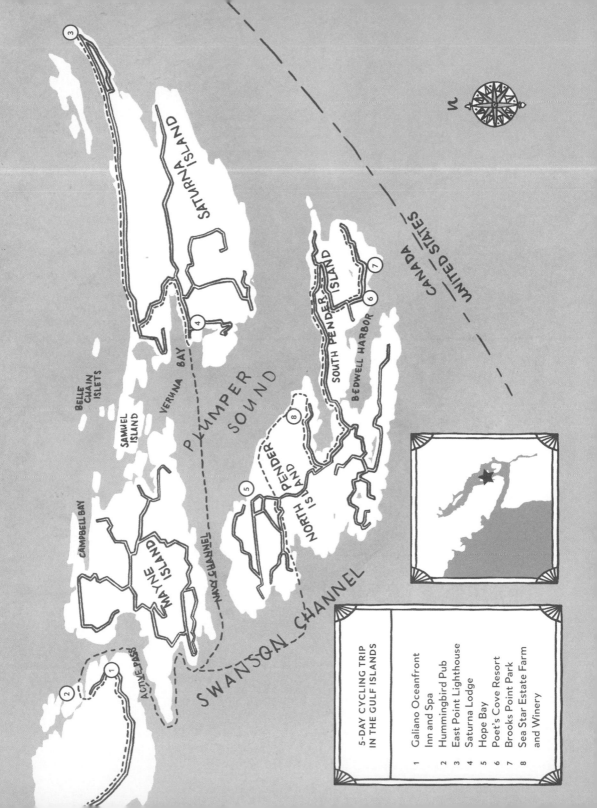

CANADA

UNITED STATES

N

SATURNA ISLAND

BELLE CHAIN ISLETS

SAMUEL ISLAND

VERUNA BAY

PLUMPER SOUND

SOUTH PENDER ISLAND

BEDWELL HARBOR

CAMPBELL BAY

MAYNE ISLAND

NAVY CHANNEL

PENDER ISLAND

NORTH ISLAND

ACTIVE PASS

SWANSON CHANNEL

5-DAY CYCLING TRIP
IN THE GULF ISLANDS

1   Galiano Oceanfront
   Inn and Spa

2   Hummingbird Pub

3   East Point Lighthouse

4   Saturna Lodge

5   Hope Bay

6   Poet's Cove Resort

7   Brooks Point Park

8   Sea Star Estate Farm
   and Winery

GEAR AND TIPS

Essential Bike Gear:
- Helmet
- Sunglasses or bike goggles for eye protection
- Front and rear lights
- Pump that fits onto your bicycle frame
- Extra tire tube and patch kit
- Under-the-seat bag to hold tire repair supplies
- Tire levers
- Small cycling toolkit with Allen wrenches
- Bicycle lock
- Emergency contact card
- Water bottle (tip: wrap several layers of duct tape around the bottle, to have on hand for quick fixes)
- Bike bell

Gear for Multiday Trips:
- Gloves
- Padded shorts
- Long-sleeved wicking-material shirt
- Panniers
- Waterproof bike jacket in a bright color and waterproof pants
- Wool sweater or fleece jacket for post-ride chill
- Waterproof shoe covers
- Maps

Tips and Tricks:
- If you do nothing else before you leave, adjust your helmet for a snug fit.
- Adjust the seat to the correct height: your heel should rest lightly on the pedal at the bottom of the stroke.
- Practice changing tires at home.
- Keep the weight of your pannier gear light. The less weight you have to carry, the easier it is to bike uphill. You will also have some room for the picnic supplies and treasures you may find.
- Line the panniers with heavy-duty trash compactor bags. Even if panniers are waterproof, they may still leak in heavy rains.
- Pace yourself up steep hills with a slow and steady cadence.
- The muscle tension built up in your legs from the workout can be relieved by pedaling easily at the summit for a few minutes before you begin the descent.
- Many lodges and hotels will keep your gear after you check out, while you cycle for the day.

There are numerous ferries from Pender Island back to Sidney and Swartz Bay. Take a late-morning boat for a leisurely 2-hour cycle back to Victoria on the Lochside Regional Trail, then catch an afternoon ferry toward home.

More Multiday Cycling Trips: Washington

Lopez and San Juan Islands | 3 days
Two reasons to explore the **San Juan Islands** by bike: you will never be shunted onto the next ferry (common with cars), and once you have paid the fare to get to an island, you can boat between islands for free.

Spencer Spit State Park on **Lopez Island** is a good place to make a cycling base camp. Bring your camp gear, or if you prefer, rent a home or cottage through Airbnb and set out from there. Spencer Spit is popular even in the fall; make reservations well in advance (bit.ly/2qsinPa). Spencer Spit also has kayak rentals if you are inclined to shake it up and get on the water. Lopez Island is the most rural and laid back of the ferry-served San Juan Islands, and biking is a joy. Spend 2 leisurely days there: have a picnic at Shark Reef Sanctuary, check out Holly B's Bakery (HollyBsBakery.com), and grab the ice cream cone with your name on it at the Just Heavenly Fudge Factory (JustHeavenlyFudge.com) in Lopez Village. Bike to Iceberg Point, park your bike, and hike out to the point, where you are likely to see seals and the occasional orca. Pick up fresh oysters and clams at Jones Family Shellfish Farm (JFFarms.com/shellfish) to throw on the campfire grill for dinner.

When you're ready to move on, catch a ferry for **San Juan Island** and cycle the northern part of the island to **Roche Harbor** and back, a 19-mile loop. Stop for wine tasting at San Juan Vineyards (SanJuanVineyards.com) along the way, and check out the Westcott Bay Sculpture Park and Nature Reserve's outdoor art sculptures. Continue on your way to elegant Roche Harbor, where there are kayak rentals, an excellent lunch at Madrona Bar and Grill (bit.ly/2upJlcN), a hotel, and hikes. You will be tempted to spend the night and could factor in a stay there if desired.

Use the HikeBikeTravel guide (bit.ly/2r6Ptsb) to find further options and detailed lists of bike routes and points of interest while biking in the San Juan Islands, including Orcas Island; it is a stretch to day cycle from Lopez to Orcas, but you may want to include it on your trip.

More Multiday Cycling Trips: Oregon

Fort Stevens State Park | 3 days

Bring the kids and bikes to Fort Stevens State Park in **Warrenton**. Fort Stevens was a military defense installation used to guard the mouth of the Columbia River from the Civil War era through World War II, and it is now transformed into a recreational playground of 4,300 acres, including 9 miles of paved bike trails. There are also hikes to take, lakes to swim in, and sand dunes to somersault down. Play hide-and-seek in the spooky turn-of-the-century gun batteries, or check out the shipwreck on the beach. Fort Stevens offers a range of overnight options—from campsites or yurts to cabins with hot showers. It also has adult bike rentals if you can't fit all the gear in your car. For reservations visit bit.ly/2t6Y9O2.

If it's raining and you are looking for some indoor alternatives, visit the exceptional Columbia River Maritime Museum (CRMM.org) in **Astoria**, and afterward make a beeline for Columbian Café (ColumbianVoodoo.com), which serves house-made jellies on artisan toast, among other fresh, local delicacies—bring cash; it doesn't take credit cards. Bring home luscious seafood souvenirs in your cooler: Dungeness crab and smoked Chinook salmon from the Skipanon Brand Seafood Store (SkipanonBrand.com) in Warrenton. Worth the stop!

ROAD TRIP: ONE SQUARE INCH OF SILENCE IN THE HOH RAIN FOREST | *3 days*

One of the quietest places in the United States is tucked into the Hoh Rain Forest on the Olympic Peninsula in Washington and is marked by a tiny red stone 3 miles from the Hoh Rain Forest Visitor Center.

Acoustic ecologist Gordon Hempton created One Square Inch of Silence (OneSquareInch.org) with hope that it would become the world's first quiet reserve. National parks are our refuge from urban racket, and Hempton's research found that in most national parks there are maybe 5 minutes of sustained silence from man-made noise like air traffic and vehicles. In the Hoh Rain Forest the silence can be up to 20 minutes long. "Silence is not the absence of something but the presence of everything," Hempton believes.

The Inch is not actually silent. The drum-thrum call of a spruce grouse, the current of the Hoh River against stones, the bugling of elk in the fall, and the drip of rain from the canopy to the understory break through the quiet, but those are sounds, not noise. Noise is background television and air traffic overhead. We are habituated to the bombardment of noise, but the moment we find ourselves in the soundscape of nature, everything changes: we relax, blood pressure drops, and we shift from screening out the clatter to drinking in the sounds.

Although the one-way, 3-mile hike from the Hoh Rain Forest Visitor Center to One Square Inch of Silence can technically be done in a single day, the Olympic Peninsula is a remote and powerful place to spend a few days exploring. Plan on 2 nights.

There are several excellent places to stay in this corner of Olympic National Park, and unless you camp out on the Hoh River Trail, all are at least an hour's drive from the Hoh Rain Forest Visitor Center, the start of the hike. Quileute Oceanside Resort in La Push (QuileuteOceanside .com), on the Quileute reservation, is closest to the trailhead, and the cabins there are set right on the beach. The resort offers a wide variety of accommodations for most budgets: RV hookups, bare-bones camper cabins, deluxe cabins, and motel rooms. Two other fabulous alternatives are the cabins at Lochaerie Resort (Lochaerie.com), and Lake Quinault Lodge (bit.ly/2b5Th0W).

CANADA
UNITED STATES

VANCOUVER ISLAND

STRAIT OF JUAN DE FUCA

PACIFIC OCEAN

⑨
⑧

SEKIU

OZETTE

PYSHT   HWY 112

JOYCE

HWY 112

HWY 101

⑪ HWY 112

①

LA PUSH

② FORKS

③

HOH RAIN FOREST

⑥

⑦

HOH RIVER

MT. OLYMPUS

QUEETS RIVER

OLYMPIC NATIONAL PARK

RIVER

④ LAKE QUINAULT
⑤

QUINAULT

TAHOLAH

HWY 101

PACIFIC BEACH

COPALIS BEACH

N

ROAD TRIP: ONE SQUARE
INCH OF SILENCE IN THE
HOH RAIN FOREST

1   Sol Duc Hot Springs
    Resort
2   Forks Outfitters Thriftway
3   Quileute Oceanside Resort
4   Lochaerie Resort
5   Lake Quinault Lodge
6   Hoh Rainforest
    Visitor Center
7   One Square Inch of Silence
8   Makah Museum, Neah Bay
9   Cape Flattery

How to Get There

Begin this road trip through the Olympic Peninsula, designated one of the most scenic drives in the United States, by catching the ferry to **Bainbridge Island** early in the morning. After driving off the ferry head to breakfast at the Madison Diner (TheMadisonDiner.com) in **Winslow**, where locals enjoy their famous corn pancakes with slabs of bacon. Follow State Route 305 north to SR 3 north in Poulsbo. Turn left (west) on SR 104 across the Hood Canal Bridge. SR 104 intersects with US Highway 101, your route to **La Push**, where you will be staying. Go north on US 101. If you make the trip before November 1, stop at Sol Duc Hot Springs Resort off US 101, approximately 113 miles from Bainbridge Island. The hot springs close for the season November 1 and reopen late March. Reset the body for the tranquility ahead and spend several hours soaking in the thermal pools. Continue on to La Push and stop to stock up on food supplies at the Forks Outfitters Thriftway (ForksOutfitters.com) for your stay. It is the last grocery store before La Push.

Fall asleep to the roar of the Pacific Ocean your first night at Quileute Oceanside Resort, and in the morning pack up a picnic, water, GPS, and rain gear (it is a *rain* forest, after all), and drive US 101 south to the Hoh Rain Forest Visitor Center turnoff. You are now entering the finest remaining section of virgin temperate rain forest in the western hemisphere, and the 12 to 14 feet of rain it receives per year make it all happen. Walk 3.2 miles from the visitor center down the Hoh River Trail through a dreamy landscape of giant western hemlock, big-leaf maple, and Sitka spruce draped in layers of ferns, lichens, and moss. These epiphytes (plants that grow upon other plants) add to the ethereal pageant of green. Use the GPS to navigate slightly off trail to N 47 51.959, W 123 52.221, and 678 feet above sea level (visit OneSquareInch .org/map to download specific landmarks to look for on the way to the site). You'll know you have arrived at the One Square Inch of Silence by a small red stone set in the moss on top of a log. Close your eyes and listen. This is what true nature sounds like.

You have several fine options for your remaining time on the peninsula:

- Hike just over a mile to wild and gorgeous **Rialto Beach** from the trailhead at the end of Mora Road in La Push. From Rialto walk the beach 1.5 miles to Hole-in-the-Wall, an iconic sea-stack arch.
- Drive to **Neah Bay** and visit the world-class tribal Makah Museum. It is a treasure of exhibits and artifacts from Makah culture, with full-size replicas of cedar dugout canoes and a longhouse. Art and baskets made by Native weavers are available in the museum gift shop.
- Explore **Cape Flattery**, the northwesternmost point in the contiguous United States. Buy the required recreational permit in Neah Bay (the Makah Museum and a few local marts sell them). Hike the 0.75-mile trail that winds though a Sitka spruce forest to three viewing platforms that overlook the Pacific Ocean. Breathe deeply. University of Washington researchers found that the air here is among the purest in the United States.
- Visit John's Beachcombing Museum in **Forks**. It started with a few glass floats in 1976 and grew to a warehouse filled with beach-found treasures, from whale skulls to the debris washed ashore from the 2011 Japanese tsunami. Worth a visit!
- Go bird-watching at **Hobuck Beach**, part of the Great Washington State Birding Trail (bit.ly/2smXgny), near Cape Flattery. Watch for storm petrels, wandering tattlers, and murrelets. Hobuck is also popular with kayakers and surfers.

PADDLE DAY TRIP: SEATTLE'S BALLARD LOCKS

The Pacific Northwest is filled with boating opportunities, but a real adventure is to take a kayak through the Hiram M. Chittenden Locks in Ballard. The locks were created to transport boats from Puget Sound to Lake Union and Lake Washington while holding the lakes' freshwater level. They were completed in 1916 and continue to this day to carry more boat traffic than any other locks in the United States. Participate in **Seattle**'s rich maritime history and paddle from Lake Union, through Salmon Bay and the locks, to Shilshole Bay for lunch, and then back. It's a grand and unforgettable experience.

You need around 6 hours for this adventure, and it is wise to start in the morning. If you don't own a kayak, there are several places on Lake Union to rent one, including Moss Bay (MossBay.co), which has a wide selection of kayaks and a friendly and knowledgeable staff. Put in at Terry Pettus Park on the east side of Lake Union where there is parking, a public dock, and shoreline access.

The route is straightforward. Check out the houseboats along Lake Union and make your way west into Salmon Bay, where large fish-processing ships and fishing boats line the docks. Look up as you pass beneath the Ballard Bridge grate; it is surreal to see the traffic pass as you serenely float under it. As you approach the locks, look for two: one lock for small boat traffic and one for larger vessels. Bear south for the smaller lock. A red-light/green-light system indicates when you may enter, with the light on the right-hand side. Green light means enter, and red means wait. If there is little boat traffic, you may have to wait for other vessels to join you. After the green light goes on and you enter, the lock attendant will instruct you which side of the lock to paddle to. Keep in mind that going into Puget Sound the water will drop, and on the return from Puget Sound to the lake, it will rise. If you happen to enter the locks on a very low tide, there will be a more robust current as the water level drops. Larger boats tie off with lines, but as a kayaker you will hold onto the gaps and cracks of the lock's wall as the water level changes; it is easier than it sounds! When the bells announce that the gates are opening into Puget Sound, wait for the call from the lock attendant for permission to paddle out.

Paddle north to Shilshole Bay Marina. There is a north entrance and a south entrance to the marina. Enter at the south entrance and paddle north to the kayak float south of the W dock; haul out there. Hungry yet? Walk 10 minutes south to Ray's Boathouse (Rays.com), head up to the café on the top deck, and order a Dungeness crab–cake sandwich and a brew. Then retrace your route back to the locks and into Lake Union.

TEMPERATE RAIN FORESTS OF THE PACIFIC NORTHWEST

The sea plays a vital role in the creation of a temperate rain forest. Warm ocean air heavy with moisture sweeps up the coastal mountains, where it cools and releases a prodigious amount of rain. Rivers, foggy mist, and heavy snowpack in the mountains also contribute to the critical levels of moisture necessary to sustain this unique biome. The temperature of the sea keeps the climate mild, with an average summer temperature of 69 degrees F and winter temperatures rarely dropping below freezing. The combination of sea, mountains, rain, and mild temperatures creates an abundance of flora and fauna, with trees stretching up to 300 feet tall, dropping needles and leaf litter that decay and make a rich bed for other plants to flourish and support wildlife.

Look for these three old-growth tree stages that can occur in temperate rain forests:

- **NURSE LOGS** are giant trees that have fallen to the forest floor. As they decay the nutrients support the growth of seedlings that often grow into trees as big as their mother.
- **STILT TREES** are saplings that have straddled the nurse log as they grew. As the log breaks down, the growing tree now has an empty space where the nurse log was; many of these spaces under the trees are big enough to walk through. Look for a spruce stilt tree near the One Square Inch of Silence.
- **COLONNADES** are lines of trees that stand single file like soldiers in a row. They have grown along the length of a nurse log and look as if they were planted in a tree farm.

STILT TREE   COLONNADES   NURSE LOG

Catch it, Cook it, Eat it

SALMON

Salmon are the quintessential fish of the Pacific Northwest and for centuries were one of the most important food sources for the Native people living in the region. Although urban development and pollution have greatly reduced salmon habitat, environmental efforts to restore declining salmon runs in Puget Sound are gaining ground. Pink and chum salmon are the poster children out of the five North Pacific species, as their numbers have increased exponentially over the past few years. Some experts say it is because they are the pigeons of the salmon world and not as sensitive to pollutants and environmental degradation, unlike king and sockeye salmon, which need clean, chemical-free water for the juveniles to survive. Salmon fishing is possible nearly year round, but check the Species Harvest Calendar for the Puget Sound Region (see page 224) for the best time to catch each species.

Where to Go
Hooking your first salmon is an unforgettable thrill, and the Pacific Northwest is the place to start. If you are new to salmon fishing, consider hiring a salmon charter boat. The professionals are keen to get you onto fish and will not only take you to where they are running, but also have the equipment and know-how to teach you the best fishing techniques. You can shorten the learning curve, have the fishing gear and tackle provided, learn where the salmon are, and put all that information to use when you are out on your own.

Tips and Tricks for Finding a Salmon Charter Boat

- Research the salmon charter company's reputation. Go online and read reviews, call the company and ask for references, then check them out.
- When you call the charter, ask these questions:
    - Does the captain also fish along with you? This is a good thing. You can learn techniques on your own fishing rod while the captain shows you how on his.
    - Are there any hidden costs in the charter fee?
    - What does the charter boat provide in terms of equipment, tackle, and bait? Are lunch and water provided?
    - How long will it take to get to the fishing grounds, and how long will you actually be fishing for?
    - Does the charter include cleaning and bagging your caught fish?
- Choose the captain, not the boat. You can have the best day of fishing in a slow, old boat, and the worst in a fancy high-end vessel. When you call you will get an idea of compatibility between you and the captain. If you are comfortable, it is a good sign the fishing experience will go well.
- Keep in mind the cheapest charter is not always best. Do your homework and check reviews online, and call the references provided.
- Whether you hire a charter or fish on your own, here are links to fishing reports for guidance on where to go:
    - BRITISH COLUMBIA: bit.ly/2tqvDtf
    - WASHINGTON: bit.ly/2t764ec
    - OREGON: bit.ly/2trMJ9R

Equipment and Technique

There are several ways to catch a salmon depending on the time of year and which run is active. A good time to sport fish for salmon in the Pacific Northwest is from late summer through early fall, when the two most targeted species, silver and king, are running. On odd numbered years, you can fish for pink salmon. The two most popular ways to catch them are trolling and mooching (a type of drift fishing) from a boat. You can also fish from a public pier, the beach, or the shore of a local river during spawning season. Whichever method you decide to use, it is always a good idea to stop by an outdoor sporting goods store to get the most up-to-date information on what the salmon are biting and where the fishing is hot. In **Seattle** a good place to start is Outdoor Emporium (SportCo.com). It has a large assortment of fishing gear and the staff is knowledgeable.

Fishing from a boat is generally the most effective, simply because you can move to where the fish are (and set crab pots at the same time if crabbing season is open). If you have never fished for salmon, consider springing for a guide. A reputable guide will work hard to help you catch fish, and you can learn a great deal about equipment, technique, and tips on where the fishing is good in your area. Then take that information and rent your own boat or, even better, join a local fishing club. You will meet passionate fishers, listen to informative speakers, and perhaps meet up with other members willing to take you out and show you the ropes. Two in the Puget Sound area are the Seattle Poggie Club (SeattlePoggies.com) and the Puget Sound Anglers (PugetSoundAnglers.org), which has chapters in many communities up and down Puget Sound. In Victoria, BC, check out the Esquimalt Anglers Association (EsquimaltAnglers.ca).

Trolling Techniques

Prepare everything you need the night before—you must be out on the fishing grounds in the dark before dawn, when the most salmon are caught. Do your research before heading out. Check here for salmon fishing updates and openings in the Puget Sound region: bit.ly/1Tw0pCF. In British Columbia: bit.ly/2t7dcar. In Oregon: bit.ly/2t74Z6a.

For your fishing trip remember to bring a license, a rod, and tackle box with spare lures, flashers, weights, hooks, and leader. Don't forget rain gear and a headlamp for the predawn dark.

- 8.5- to 9-foot rod rated for 15- to 30-pound line
- 8-ounce kidney weight with swivels
- 6 feet of leader line
- Flasher
- Double hook for the herring
- Lure
- Downrigger

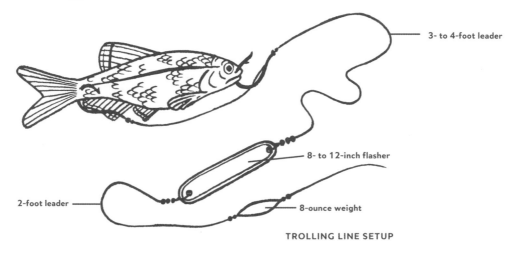

3- to 4-foot leader

8- to 12-inch flasher

2-foot leader

8-ounce weight

TROLLING LINE SETUP

Getting the bait or lure to the right depth is key for trolling successfully. The best way to do this is by using a downrigger, a device that lowers a large, usually 10-pound, weight to your desired depth, with your line attached to it with a quick-release clip. When a fish strikes, the line releases from the downrigger clip, and you can play the fish unencumbered. Kings typically run deeper than silvers, usually below 40 feet, and a downrigger is necessary for targeting them. If you are fishing for silvers, using a line with a weight is a fine option. For a useful guide to using downriggers check out this YouTube video: bit.ly/2sWStYw.

To set up for trolling, rig the line in this order: First tie an 8-ounce weight to the main line, then run 2 feet of leader line from the weight and tie on a flasher; next tie on 3 or 4 feet of leader from the flasher, and knot the double hooks on the line with a snell knot (see bit.ly/2ssJCdF). Hook the herring through the body as illustrated on page 85 or tie on a lure recommended by a local tackle shop.

Trolling speed is very important. For kings, try to hold boat speed to 1 to 3 knots. For silvers, troll a bit faster—3 to 5 knots. Regardless of speed, make sure your herring or lure has good action before you lower it. A herring or lure that doesn't jerk or rotate in the current will not entice a bite. It can be difficult to gauge the depth of your tackle if you are not using a downrigger, but a good rule of thumb is to let out about 50 to 70 feet of line with a weighted setup. If you want to fish deeper, adding a heavier weight is more effective than playing out more line. Check your lure every 15 minutes to ensure the action is still good and isn't fouled by seaweed.

Mooching Techniques

Drift fishing is fishing from a boat without using the motor. You drift fish when you don't have to chase the salmon and they are running in high concentrations. Mooching, a type of drift fishing, is a dying art in the salmon-fishing world. The gear is straightforward, the silent drift with no motor is peaceful, and using a real herring cut to a perfect bevel instead of using a lure is considered by some fishers a purist's approach to salmon fishing. Simply put, mooching is fishing with a banana-shaped weight that pulls the line down to the depth you want, along with a fresh herring (or a herring brined in salt water for firmness) with the head beveled at precise angles, causing the herring to spin, both rising and falling, attracting a hungry salmon.

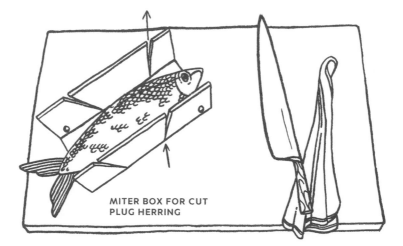

MITER BOX FOR CUT
PLUG HERRING

NORTH PACIFIC SALMON

There are five species of native North Pacific salmon in the genus *Oncorhynchus* (see Handy Guide to the Five Species of North Pacific Salmon on page 91). Each of them has two, sometimes three names, which can be confusing. Here's a guide to the species along with the best months for fishing them. Always check fish and game regulations in your area before fishing to make sure there is an opening.

- CHUM (dog, keta), September through November: Chums are considered the least tasty and least valuable salmon on the market. Some say the name "dog salmon" comes from Alaskans who would catch the plentiful fish, dry it, and feed it to their sled dogs during the winter. Even so, it is a delicious high-protein fish. Today the salmon industry is marketing chums with the more palatable name "keta." They are also sometimes called silverbrites. Chum roe eggs are the most valuable roe out of the five varieties, known for their delicate flavor and large size.

- SOCKEYE (reds, blueback), August through September: Sockeyes are the most important commercial species of all the North Pacific salmon. They are a beautiful salmon with rich red flesh and a high oil content. They are one of the smaller salmon, with only pinks being smaller. They make their way from the sea up streams and rivers to spawn in lakes.

- KING (Chinook, tyee, blackmouth), July through August: The granddaddy and most prized of the five, they are also the least abundant. Kings are the largest of the wild salmon, with the world record weighing in at 97 pounds. They generally run over 25 pounds. Their succulent flesh, high oil content, and firm texture make kings a cook's dream fish. Blackmouth are immature king salmon that hang around inland waters instead of heading out to sea.

- SILVER (coho), July through September: Swift and aggressive, these are a favorite of anglers to catch. They tend to congregate at the mouths of rivers before heading upstream, making them easier to target.

- PINK (humpy, humpback), July through September: Pinks, the most abundant salmon, have pale flesh that is light in texture, making the fish easy for even finicky kids to eat. Pinks spawn every 2 years, creating two types: odd-year pinks and even-year pinks. British Columbia and the Puget Sound region produce odd-year pinks. Pinks are also called humpies for the large back hump that grows on males during the spawning migration.

- 8.5- or 9-foot rod with a level wind or baitcasting reel with 14- to 20-pound line
- 4-ounce banana or kidney weight with a beaded swivel
- 6 feet of leader line with two hooks tied on with snell knot
- Fresh or brined herring
- Miter box specifically for cut plug herring (it takes the guesswork out of the angles)

Tie the weight to the end of the main line, with the bead swivel end down toward the hook. The swivel allows the leader to spin without twisting the main line. Next tie on the leader with the hooks. Bevel the herring using the miter box. To secure the cut plug herring, hook the front hook in through the belly and out the top of the backbone. Leave the other hook to dangle.

Drop the herring down and let the tide carry the bait along, or drop down and reel up one handle crank at a time, pausing between cranks about 15 to 20 seconds. As soon as you feel a bump, set the hook with an upward movement of the rod. Play the salmon by setting the tension on the reel so the fish can run, then reel it in slowly, and scoop it into the boat with a net.

Beach Salmon-Fishing Techniques

Two species of Pacific salmon travel close to shore in the inland waters of the Salish Sea, where you can catch them, at the end of their saltwater phase: coho and pinks. In the Puget Sound region the pink salmon run happens on odd years. Every odd year (2019, for example) they return to spawn after spending 2 years at sea. Silvers run every year from the sea to their natal spawning grounds.

GEAR FOR BEACH CASTING
- Spinning rod and reel
- 10- to 15-pound line
- 0.5- to 1-ounce weight
- Pink buzz bomb or twitching jig
- Barrel swivel

From shore cast out to the trough (the drop-off that most beaches have), which is where the salmon hang out. Let the lure sink until it nears the bottom, then jig it back in with quick jerks, moving the rod tip up about a foot. When the tip is low, reel in the slack. Instantly set the hook with an upward jerk when you feel a bite. Here's a link to great information for successful shore fishing: bit.ly/2u35EYw.

Tips and Tricks

- Drift or troll in the boat *with* the tide, not against it. Salmon face into the tidal current, making it easier for them to see your lure.
- Pink salmon love pink lures.
- Salt water is corrosive to your fishing gear. Rinse everything in fresh water when you are finished, including the lures and the reel. Dry with a soft cloth.
- Salmon feed best in low light: overcast days, dawn, and dusk are optimal times to catch them. On bright, sunny days they are less active and hang out in deeper water.
- Don't be shy and ask for help from experienced fishers. Local knowledge can give you an edge on snagging a salmon.
- Net the salmon headfirst. Fish don't swim backward, and you want to ensure it swims forward into the net.

HANDY GUIDE TO THE FIVE SPECIES
OF NORTH PACIFIC SALMON

Everyone who lives in the Pacific Northwest should know the five species of North Pacific salmon. All you need is your five fingers to remember them.

THUMB: Chum, for "chumming" a ride
INDEX FINGER: Sockeye, because it's #1!
MIDDLE FINGER: King, the biggest salmon and the longest finger on your hand
RING FINGER: Silver, the finger for your silver ring
PINKIE FINGER: Pink, the smallest salmon and shortest finger on your hand

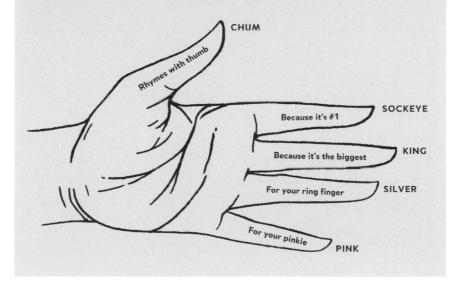

Campfire Cedar-Planked Salmon

Salmon grilled on a soaked cedar plank is divine. The process retains moisture and the cedar infuses the fillet with its inimitable Northwest flavor. Buy a cedar plank at a grocery store or lumber store (three-quarters inch thick, eight inch by eight inch; be sure it is untreated, and cut it to size). You can grill over an open fire using a camp grill or use a gas barbecue grill. Feel free to soak the plank in different liquids such as cider or wine.

INGREDIENTS:

1 (14.9-ounce) can Guinness draught beer

2 tablespoons extra-virgin olive oil

1 (2-pound) salmon fillet, skin on

Kosher salt and freshly ground black pepper

½ lemon, cut into thin rounds

2 tablespoons finely chopped fresh dill

Place the cedar plank in a rimmed baking sheet and pour the beer over it. Soak for 8 hours. If using a campfire, an hour before you start grilling, build the campfire (see How to Build a Bonfire, page 60) and let it burn down to coals. Place the camp grill over the coals. If using a gas grill, pre-heat it to about 350 degrees F or a medium heat setting. Rub the olive oil over the salmon, sprinkle with salt and pepper, and lay the lemon slices over it. Remove the plank from the beer, and lay it on the grill. Place the salmon skin side down onto the cedar plank. Fill a spray bottle with water and keep it handy to douse any flames that rear up (this is normal, especially over a campfire). Grill for about 15 minutes, or until the salmon is uniformly pink. Sprinkle with dill, and serve.

Salmon Burgers with Tarragon

MAKES 6 SERVINGS

Salmon burgers are a luscious way to use salmon. Do not use a food processor to dice the salmon; overprocessing the flesh makes it tough. You can make the burger mix ahead of time; store in a glass bowl, covered, up to twenty-four hours in the refrigerator.

INGREDIENTS:

2 pounds skinless salmon fillet

⅓ cup plain full-fat Greek yogurt

1 cup dry, unseasoned fine bread crumbs

2 tablespoons freshly squeezed lemon juice

4 green onions (white and green parts), minced

1 medium red bell pepper (about 6 ounces), cut into ¼-inch dice

2 tablespoons fresh chopped tarragon

1 teaspoon salt

1 tablespoon salted butter, for frying

6 sourdough buns

6 slices fresh tomato

6 slices red onion

Tartar sauce, for serving

Dice the salmon into ¼- to ½-inch pieces. In a large bowl, add the salmon, yogurt, bread crumbs, and lemon juice. Add the green onions, bell pepper, tarragon, and salt, and mix thoroughly. Shape into 6 patties.

Melt the butter in a heavy-bottomed frying pan over medium-low heat. Add the patties without crowding them and fry for 5 to 7 minutes, or until nicely browned. Flip and cook 5 to 7 more minutes. Serve on the buns with 1 slice of tomato and red onion per sandwich, and tartar sauce on the side.

Sunday Salmon Chowder

MAKES 4 TO 6 SERVINGS

This salmon chowder is a Sunday feast when served with a salad and loaf of crusty sourdough bread. Smoky and creamy notes balance with the chunks of salmon, and clam juice intensifies the seafood flavors.

INGREDIENTS:

3 tablespoons unsalted butter, cut into 3 pieces

1 teaspoon fennel seeds, crushed with a mortar and pestle or the end of a rolling pin

1 medium leek (about 6 ounces, white and light-green parts only), cut in half and thinly sliced

2 tablespoons unbleached all-purpose flour

2 (8-ounce) bottles clam juice

3 cups water

5 medium red potatoes (about 1½ pounds), cut into ½-inch dices

2 ribs celery (about 4 ounces), cut into ¼-inch dice

4 strips thick smoked bacon, cut and cooked until crisp

1 quart half-and-half

2 pounds skinless salmon fillet, cut into ½-inch cubes

Kosher salt and freshly ground black pepper

In a large stockpot over medium-low heat, melt the butter. Add the fennel seeds, stir for a few seconds, then add the leeks. Sauté until the leeks are nearly soft, 5 to 8 minutes, stirring occasionally. Sprinkle the flour over the leeks, and cook, stirring occasionally, for 2 to 3 more minutes. Slowly whisk in the clam juice and water, and bring to a simmer. Add the potatoes and celery, bring to a simmer, and cook until soft, 8 to 10 minutes. Add the bacon and half-and-half, and stir to combine. Gently add the salmon, and simmer until the salmon is just cooked through; it will only take 2 to 3 minutes. Take care not to bring the chowder to a rolling boil after adding the half-and-half, or it will separate and become grainy. Add salt and pepper to taste, and serve immediately.

MICRO-ADVENTURE: FORAGE

Take a class on chanterelles and head to the woods to hunt for these delectable Northwest mushrooms. Chanterelles begin to appear after the first heavy rain at the end of summer and continue until the first frost. Here are some excellent resources for learning more about foraging in the Northwest:

British Columbia
- Swallow Tail tours: bit.ly/1k7llQc
- Deerholme Farm wild food foraging: bit.ly/2sXCpFV
- Vancouver Mycological Society: VanMyco.com

Washington
- The Field Trip Society: bit.ly/2qz3knR
- Langdon Cook: LangdonCook.com/Classes
- Puget Sound Mycological Society: bit.ly/2ri6FsO
- Seattle Tilth: bit.ly/2qyKY6E
- Bainbridge Island foraging classes: BiParks.org/Outdoor

Oregon
- Oregon Mycological Society: WildMushrooms.org

Beach Projects

SEASHORE FOSSILS

Choose your fossil (shells, crab carapaces, sticks, leaves, or your own feet) and use plaster of paris to preserve it for a glimpse of the past.

WHAT YOU WILL NEED:
Plaster of paris
Water
Bucket
Stick, for stirring
Shells, crab carapaces, sticks, leaves, or your own feet
Petroleum jelly

Mix the plaster of paris and water in the bucket, using a stick, according to the package's directions; you can use seawater. Coat the shell or other items lightly with petroleum jelly. Dig a shallow depression into the sand and place the item in the hole, petroleum jelly side up. Alternatively, if you are using your own foot, make a footprint in damp sand. Pour the prepared plaster into the depression.

Wait until the plaster sets—depending on the ambient temperature, this can take anywhere from less than 1 to several hours (cooler weather will slow the hardening process). Then lift the hardened plaster from the sand and remove the shell or other item.

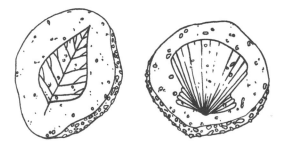

HERBED SEA SALT

MAKES ABOUT 1 CUP

Making your own sea salt is an easy if time-consuming process. To avoid contaminants, collect the seawater away from freshwater runoff and avoid seawater near city beaches if possible. Your best bet is a scoop from the Pacific Ocean. If you find yourself traveling down the Oregon coast near Netarts Bay, check out Ben Jacobsen's Sea Salt Company (JacobsenSalt.com). His process is meticulous and slow and produces some of the best sea salt available in the United States.

WHAT YOU WILL NEED:
1 gallon seawater
Clean bucket
Cheesecloth, cut to fit into the sieve with some overlap
Sieve
Large pot (the shallower it is, the faster the water will evaporate)
Shallow baking sheet
Parchment paper
2 tablespoons finely chopped fresh herbs (rosemary, oregano, mint, tarragon, or a mix)

On the beach, scoop a gallon of clean seawater into the bucket and let it sit for an hour to allow any sediment to settle to the bottom.

At home, place the cheesecloth into the sieve and pour the seawater through it into the pot to collect any remaining particles. Bring the seawater to a boil over high heat, and boil for several hours until it is reduced to around 3 inches. While the water is boiling, line the baking sheet with parchment paper and set aside. The trick to making sea salt is not to scorch it, and it is easy to scorch if you turn your back when it gets down to the last few inches of water. At that time you will see the salt grains begin to form at the bottom of the pan.

Turn the heat down to medium high, and stir continuously until the solution begins to resemble wet sand. Do not evaporate all the water. When it is thick with salt but still pourable, you are done. Remove the pot from the heat, pour the salt onto the prepared baking sheet, and air-dry

CONTINUED

for 3 to 5 days, stirring it up occasionally. You can speed up the process if you have a food dehydrator by pouring the solution on the parchment paper and placing it in the dehydrator on low heat for several hours. This will produce a finer, more powdery salt, while a slower air-drying time produces a flakier salt. When the salt is dry, mix in the fresh herbs and place the salt in clean jars, where it will keep indefinitely.

ROCK CAIRNS

For thousands of years people have built rock cairns to indicate their paths and find their way home. Today cairns are trail markers, landmarks, or art as symbols of human intention. Explore rock cairns with a visit to the Earth Sanctuary retreat on Whidbey Island, where paths are punctuated with them—from large megaliths of balanced stones to the Zen impermanence of small towers that will eventually tip and spill. To build your own, use a variety of rock sizes from large to small; flat rocks are easiest to begin with.

WHAT YOU WILL NEED:
Smooth, rounded rocks
Patience

Begin with a stable foundation for the cairn, a wide and flat rock. Think *center of gravity* as you slowly and patiently place rocks on top of the first one. Test that center of gravity as you place each rock; it can shift with the weight of the upper rocks and need adjustment. If the weight is unstable, shift the rock incrementally until it seems to shoulder the load. As you grow bolder, experiment with stones of unusual shapes to find the contact points for the stones to balance.

FISH PRINTS

The Japanese call it gyotaku, *an ancient technique fishers used to record their catch. You can use previously frozen and thawed fish for this project; don't plan on eating the fish after printing.*

WHAT YOU WILL NEED:

1 whole fish, skin on

Juice of 1 lemon

Paper towels

Baking sheet

Water-soluble block printing ink

Shallow plate

Brayer (a roller, for spreading ink)

Sumi rice paper

A clean fish allows the ink to stick better. Begin by removing the slime from the side of the fish you want to print, using the lemon juice and paper towels; pat it dry. Lay the fish on the baking sheet. For full ink coverage, spread the fins and place wadded-up paper towels underneath them to raise them up. Squirt some ink in the shallow plate, and roll the brayer back and forth across it to cover the roller in ink. Roll the brayer evenly over the body and fins until one side is lightly covered. Place the rice paper over the fish and gently rub the paper with your fingers. Peel off the paper. There it is, a beautiful fish print! Discard the fish, and wash the brayer and plate with water for a simple cleanup.

On the Water

SURFING

You might not normally associate surfing with the cold waters of the Pacific Northwest, but it is becoming increasingly more popular with the Pacific's shapely wave peaks, the proliferation of surf schools, and the miles of sandy beaches. You have to wear a wet suit to protect yourself against the cold water, but there are enough waves to go around—from user-friendly beginner swells to long beach breaks. Surfing in autumn has the ideal combination of summer's gentle waves with an early-winter swell nosing in to make things interesting. Learn to surf in the Pacific Northwest, and you can surf anywhere.

Tofino

The gradual slope of the continental shelf, the wide sandy beaches, and the warm and lively village of **Tofino** make surfing here on British Columbia's **Vancouver Island** an ideal adventure. Going with friends or partners who don't surf? There are plenty of outdoor alternatives when you are not hitting the waves: exploring Hot Springs Cove, hiking, biking, kayaking, and canoeing are only a few of the options. Check to see if the West Coast Weird Off is being held, usually in September. This all-day event celebrates surfing at its goofiest with costumes, alternative surf craft, and an Anything but a Board division. This is not the classic contest of the best cut or the longest barrel, but "a super duper anti-contest for the warm hearted and cold footed" sponsored by the Cold Feet Club (Facebook.com/ColdFeetClub).

There are many surf shops and schools offering everything you need. Here are a few to get you started:

- **LONG BEACH SURF SHOP**: LongBeachSurfShop.com
- **PACIFIC SURF SCHOOL**: PacificSurfSchool.com
- **WESTSIDE SURF SCHOOL**: WestSideSurf.com
- **SURF SISTER SURF SCHOOL**: SurfSister.com
- **TOFINO SURF ADVENTURES**: TofinoSurfAdventures.ca

SURFING TIPS AND TRICKS

- Start with a long soft-top board. It is stable and grippy for the feet.
- Do research, read reviews, and pick a skilled instructor. A good teacher will support and inspire you through the learning curve.
- Make safe choices. If a wave looks too big for you, it probably is.
- Follow the rule of one surfer at a time on a wave. The surfer closest to the point where the wave breaks has the right-of-way.
- When you paddle out past the break to other surfers, join the line and take your turn. It is poor etiquette to take the first available wave when there are others waiting.
- Don't paddle close to someone ready and in position to catch a wave.
- Stay perpendicular to the wave when paddling out to a break. Duck under it or paddle over it. When you are at an angle to it, there is more body surface area for the wave to drag you down.
- Avoid a collision. Look both ways along the break before taking off.
- Once you are upright, steer with your eyes. Where the eyes go, energy flows.
- Increase stability by bending your knees and keeping your center of gravity low.

Learning to surf means wiping out over and over again. You will get sucked into waves, churned and burned, and thrown to shore. You will fall some more. It is all part of the learning curve, and then, when the magic moment arrives and you are upright and flying across a curl of water, life is beautiful.

Best Surfing Beaches

- **MACKENZIE BEACH**: Protected from the pounding of the Pacific Ocean by a few islands, this beach is great for kids learning to ride a wave.
- **CHESTERMAN BEACH**: This beach is rated as one of the best beaches for beginners in the Pacific Northwest.
- **COX BAY**: Even though this beach is exposed to the Pacific, a gentle beach grade creates a variety of waves for everyone from the novice to the experienced surfer.
- **LONG BEACH**: Just like its name, this lovely beach stretches for miles and is situated halfway between Ucluelet and Tofino.

Westport

Westport is one of Washington's best places to surf. It is located at the tip of **Grays Harbor** and faces the North Pacific swells that create some of the most consistently rideable waves in Washington. Westport has easy-to-access surf beaches and plenty of infrastructure with several surf shops, accommodations, cafés, bistros, and breweries. Westport is the first land the North Pacific storms run into, and the sea can throw anything at you, but with three surfing beaches near town to choose from, there is always a breaking wave to ride somewhere.

For lessons and gear, check out:

- **STEEPWATER SURF SHOP**: SteepWaterSurfShop.com
- **BIGFOOT SURF**: BigFootSurf.com
- **THE SURF SHOP**: WestportSurfShop.com

Northern Oregon Coast

There are 363 miles of public coastline in Oregon and every mile is available to surfers. When the waves are big, particularly in winter, they are epic and eaten up by veterans, and when the seas drop to sweet swells in summer, they are perfect for beginners. Surfers can thank the northern influence of the Gulf of Alaska for this. Northern Oregon's irregular coastline also means that the shore's beaches face multiple directions and the chance of finding a decent set of waves to ride doesn't depend on wind direction, one of the factors in forming good surfing waves.

When driving west down US Highway 26 to the coast, near mile marker 28, you will see a blue sign that says "Drinking Water." Stop there and fill your water bottles with some of the purest and best spring water you will ever taste. People drive from Portland to fill their water jugs with this delicious mineral water from a natural spring.

Try these surf schools and shops:

- NORTHWEST WOMEN'S SURF CAMP (SEASIDE): NWWomensSurfCamps.com
- OREGON SURF ADVENTURES (SEASIDE): OregonSurfAdventures.com
- CLEANLINE SURF (SEASIDE AND CANNON BEACH): CleanLineSurf.com
- CANNON BEACH SURF (CANNON BEACH): bit.ly/2rx60DS

Best Surfing Beaches

- INDIAN BEACH: A scenic beach 1.5 miles north of **Cannon Beach** in Ecola State Park, favored by intermediate surfers.
- SHORT SANDS BEACH (OSWALD WEST STATE PARK): Ten miles south of Cannon Beach, this popular beginner beach is also one of the most stunning and well worth checking out, whether you surf or not. Don't leave valuables in the car.
- OCEANSIDE: An all-levels beach 11 miles west of **Tillamook** with solid breaks when the conditions stack up.

Celebrations & Nature

LABOR DAY BEACHSIDE FAMILY REUNION

We often remember two things most vividly from childhood: family vacations and time spent outdoors. A beachside family reunion is both and can create enduring memories for multiple generations. Where else will you hear papa's bear story? Play cards with three generations around a table? Belly laugh with siblings or cousins over childhood escapades? Memories are priceless, and there is no rewind.

Tips and Tricks
- Plan 6 months to a year in advance, particularly if your family has a large number of people.
- Ask for help; even better, create a reunion committee and assign specific tasks: reserving the place for the event, researching activities in the area, planning games and activities, making T-shirts, et cetera. Have someone set up a Facebook page to keep everyone in the loop without having to deal with a landslide of emails and phone calls.
- Choose your place wisely. Location can make or break a reunion, and you want to accommodate all ages and stages. The beauty of a reunion by the shore is that there is something for everyone—athletes, families with young children, singles, and the elderly. The beach can hold the interests of all. Check out the places that follow for ideas. Remember to keep it affordable, with a range of options for those on fixed incomes as well as those willing to pay for more comfortable accommodation. If necessary, consider scholarships or fundraisers to help cover reunion expenses for those who are financially strapped.
- Plan a few activities over the weekend that involve all family members—meals, a card tournament, or sand castle competition, for example. Find games that teams can play rather than pitting individuals against each other. Research *Minute to Win It* games on the internet for some fast, fun ideas.

- Come up with a code word or phrase that all agree to that signals everyone to drop inflammatory topics or old battles.

The Don'ts:
- Don't try to organize a reunion alone. Asking other family members for help pulls them into the process and allows them to emotionally invest in the gathering.
- Don't bring up old grievances. It can be tempting to air a grudge in the name of being authentic, but don't do it. Family reunions are not the place or the time.
- Don't drink too much. Getting drunk is a fast track to embarrassing behavior, inappropriate comments, and hurt feelings.
- Don't be a cheapskate. We all have family members who never seem to have their purse or wallet with them, who skimp on contributions, and who never chip in when the hat is passed. Provide estimates of costs and expectations of how they will be paid beforehand. Come up with a fair way to divide the bills and share the expenses.
- Don't check texts, online news, emails, Twitter, Facebook, et cetera when you are in the company of others. Make your necessary phone calls and check-ins away from the festivities. *No one has fond memories of technological check-ins.* You will remember the goofy asides, the conversations, the sharing of family stories.
- Don't make too many rules. It is supposed to be a lovefest, not a classroom.
- Don't make too many plans. The best family reunions are the ones that allow for detours and distractions, and make room for enjoying the company and conversations.

Here are some ideas of places for your beachside family reunion. Most have a community room in case of rain, plenty of beaches, and a range of accommodations from camping to cabins to houses.

British Columbia

Yellow Point Lodge
Make your reservations early! This rustic retreat south of **Nanaimo** on **Vancouver Island** is popular and fills well in advance. Stay in the cabins or in rooms in the lodge. Yellow Point has a large saltwater swimming pool, tennis courts, bicycles, and kayaks for their guests. The feeding of the crowd is taken care of—meals are included in the room rate, in addition to three teatimes a day with homemade goodies. To get to Yellow Point Lodge, you can take Washington State Ferries from Anacortes to Sidney until September 30, or the Black Ball Ferry from Port Angeles to Victoria, or the BC Ferry in Tsawwassen to Nanaimo (Duke Point). Yellow Point Lodge requires guests to be 14 years of age and up. YellowPointLodge.com

Washington

Fort Worden State Park
You can't do better than Fort Worden for a family reunion. There is a wide variety of accommodation—comfortable officer-housing homes, cottages, retreat housing with bunks, dormitories, and camping, with plenty of ADA-compliant places. There are 2 miles of sandy beaches, plus hikes, history, and a marine science center. Add the charming town of **Port Townsend** to the mix, with its restaurants, galleries, and large marina, and you have something for everyone. You can kayak, fish, hike, clam for your dinner, and get lost in the historic military bunkers, where hide-and-seek takes on a whole different dimension (bring flashlights!). The park also has indoor meeting spaces for your group to gather together in one space. Fort Worden is hands down one of the top choices for a family reunion of any size and for all ages. FortWorden.org/Stay-Here

Cape Disappointment State Park

Cape Disappointment State Park, near **Ilwaco**, is 1,882 acres along the Pacific Ocean with old-growth forests, freshwater lakes, two lighthouses, and hiking trails. It is another spectacular place for a family reunion that will appeal to all ages. If you are lucky, the summer concert series at Waikiki Beach Amphitheater within the park will be going on (see page 64) for an unforgettable evening of music. There are ten yurts with heat, electricity, and furniture, with camp-style cooking outdoors, as well as a partially covered deck and a fire pit. There are also lovely lighthouse keepers' residences available to rent that sleep six or camping for outdoor enthusiasts. Check out the Lewis and Clark Interpretive Center, and for extra fun bring bikes and fishing gear. bit.ly/2rqu516

Willow Pond Lodge and Lake House

Willow Pond Lodge and Lake House (WillowPondLodge.com) is a luxury high-bank waterfront retreat on **Whidbey Island** with two gorgeous homes: the Lodge, which sleeps thirteen, and the Lake House, which sleeps eighteen. Both homes have large kitchens and spacious dining rooms for cooking and eating together. In addition there is a retreat center for an all-family event room. There is no option for camping on site. Whidbey Island offers fishing, hiking, and wine-tasting outings, and there is a bowling alley in **Oak Harbor** if you want to have an all-ages tournament. OakBowl.com

Oregon

Cape Lookout State Park

This gem of a park near **Tillamook** is nestled in a lush coastal rain forest and encompasses a long, sandy spit facing the Pacific Ocean. There is a wide variety of accommodations, including cabins, campsites, and RV hookup sites. Reluctant campers will enjoy the yurts, which feel like camping with furniture and heat (no kitchens—there are picnic tables and fire pits outdoors). The nearby town of Tillamook has a bowling alley and a golf course for fierce and fun family tournaments, as well as a Saturday farmers' market to collect ingredients for the all-family feast. Visit the Tillamook Cheese Factory for a tour and ice cream cones. bit.ly/2qP46fC

SALMON WATCHING AT THE LOCKS

Pacific salmon are anadromous—they hatch in freshwater, make their way to the sea, and at the end of their life cycle return to freshwater to spawn. The Ballard Locks (BallardLocks.org) in **Seattle** are a critical link both for migrating salmon moving between salt and freshwater to spawn, and for the smolts making their way to sea to live for several years. Originally the locks blocked the salmon migration into the Cedar River watershed until shortly after construction, when the US Army Corps of Engineers modified the locks and built a series of ten steps for the fish to reach their natal spawning grounds. The fish ladder was rebuilt in 1976 with twenty-one steps to aid the salmon migration. You can watch this epic annual event up close through viewing windows as the fish move through the steps, or weirs. Salmon viewing at the locks is possible from May through November, but each species has its peak viewing time.

- KINGS: July through November, peaking in late August
- SILVERS: August through November, peaking in late September
- SOCKEYES: May through October, peaking in July
- STEELHEAD: Late February through March, peaking in late March

While watching adult salmon move through the steps, observe the tiny salmon smolts moving through the locks to Puget Sound in the opposite direction. They will spend most of their lives at sea, and if they survive, they will return to spawn in the lakes and rivers of the Cedar River watershed. Their mortality rate is high. Millions of smolt hatch, but only a handful survive to spawn. They must battle natural predators, flooding, fishers, and low stream flows. They also face environmental degradation such as shoreline developments that silt the water, and poor water quality from storm-water runoff and industrial pollutants. Watching the beautiful adult fish that endured against all odds to fight their way toward spawning grounds is a moving tribute to survival.

Festivals & Events

FALL SALMON DERBIES

You can find a salmon derby somewhere in the Pacific Northwest almost year round, but fall is the best time for silvers and kings. In the late 1990s, tournaments and derbies that focused on kings disappeared when four stocks of wild king salmon were listed as threatened under the Endangered Species Act. To increase their numbers, federal and state agencies as well as several treaty tribes began clipping the adipose fin, the small fatty fin between the dorsal fin and the tail, of hatchery-produced silvers and kings. This helped anglers to distinguish hatchery salmon from wild ones and to release the latter; wild king salmon began to reappear and the derbies returned. Today salmon derbies play a vital role of encouraging boaters and anglers to harvest fish responsibly.

CITIZEN SCIENCE: MONITOR MARINE RESOURCES AND ECOSYSTEM HEALTH

Coastal Observation and Seabird Survey Team (COASST) is a network of citizen scientists on the West Coast that surveys local beaches each month for beached birds, marine debris, and evidence of human use of the beach. The COASST program originally started to provide a baseline from which a disaster like an oil spill could be assessed. To participate, volunteers attend a 6-hour COASST training session, sign a contract agreeing to survey a beach of their choice every month, and pay a small fee for survey supplies. For more information, visit Depts.Washington.edu/coast.

If you are bit by the salmon-fishing bug, entering a derby will test your luck and skills against other anglers. For more information on seasonal salmon derbies in your area, go to bit.ly/2sfSu7y. Here are a few of dozens of derbies up and down the Salish Sea to whet your appetite.

British Columbia

Port Alberni | *Port Alberni Salmon Fest*
Held Labor Day weekend, this 4-day event on **Vancouver Island** includes large cash prizes, a barbecued salmon feed, fireworks, and a Bavarian beer garden. Something for everyone! SalmonFestival.ca

Washington

Everett | *Everett Coho Derby*
Held the first weekend in November, this derby is one in the Northwest Salmon Derby Series, a program designed to protect and enhance wild stocks of kings and silvers. EverettCohoDerby.com

Seattle | *Tengu Blackmouth Derby*
Barred from fish tournaments, Japanese Americans released from internment camps in December 1946 started their own, the Tengu Blackmouth Derby. It remains one of the oldest and most revered derbies up and down the Sound in part because only the fine art of mooching is allowed (see page 87)—no artificial lures, flashers, downriggers, or hoochies. The tournament is open to all and runs for ten to twelve consecutive Sundays from October through December out of the Seacrest Boathouse in **West Seattle**, where you can rent a boat if you don't have one and head out. The derby runs during lousy weather, poor fishing, and in some years narrow legal fish boundaries, but that does not stop the enthusiasm and fierce love of hooking a blackmouth. bit.ly/2tqEpaT

Oregon

Brookings | Slam'n Salmon Ocean Derby
This 3-day derby, the largest ocean fishing derby on the West Coast, lures hundreds of fishers to try their luck at snagging the trophy king. It is held Labor Day weekend. bit.ly/2s7PVnI

Bandon | Bandon Salmon Derby
The tournament starts the day after Labor Day and ends the Friday before Columbus Day. bit.ly/2tvLYNO

PORT TOWNSEND FILM FESTIVAL

Port Townsend is a stunning town worth visiting any time of year, but if you make it to the Port Townsend Film Festival in mid-September, you are in for a splendid weekend of entertainment and inspiration. The setting is gorgeous, with the festival held on the waterfront in the National Historic Landmark District, and best of all you can walk to films ranging from cutting edge to world premiere to quirky—including documentaries, narratives, and shorts. The mission of the Port Townsend Film Festival is to connect audiences with filmmakers, and a majority of the latter attend and offer a Q&A after the film, happy to be spending the weekend rubbing shoulders with their audience.

Every night of the festival a family-friendly outdoor show is offered with straw bales for seats. For adults, there is the hugely popular Area 51, the festival bar, on the dock, serving signature locally sourced cocktails in a historic building on the waterfront. All passes include a yearlong festival membership with access to the film library, which has a breadth of films to choose from. Reserve accommodation early; it is a popular weekend in Port Townsend. Additionally, many people stay on their boats in the harbor. PTFilmFest.com

BELLINGHAM SEAFEAST

SeaFeast celebrates **Bellingham**'s world-class seafood industry and working waterfront for a weekend in late September or early October that is not to be missed. It begins with fisherpoet workshops for learning how to spin a sea tale and write a ballad or an ode. Later that afternoon the poets showcase their work at Boundary Bay Brewery (bit.ly/2s84cAJ). Learn how to prepare your favorite seafood (fillet a fish or crack and clean a crab), and watch an oyster shuck-and-slurp contest (one winner opened and ate 24 oysters in 2 minutes). The weekend is filled with art, music, fabulous seafood, free boat rides, tours of the processing plants, and a survival-suit race—an awkward swim with participants wearing the cumbersome survival suit. It is a fun Northwest celebration that brings the bounty of the sea, the fishers who harvest it, and the consumer together, and sets the people dancing in the streets to local bands. BellinghamSeaFeast.com.

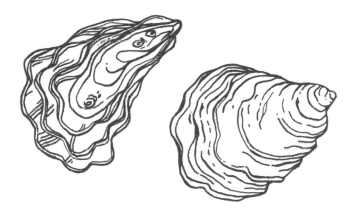

WINTER

Outings

WINTER STORM-WATCHING GETAWAYS

There are huge waves pounding the shore out there while you watch through salt-sprayed windows from the warmth of a snug room, sipping a glass of wine. This is winter in the Pacific Northwest in all its gray and stormy glory. If you can't get out of the season, get into it and immerse yourself in the lashing fury of a winter storm on the Pacific Coast.

Tofino

The first storm-watching place of choice is **Tofino** on Vancouver Island, some say the birthplace of storm watching, an idea cooked up by locals of this formerly one-season resort town, who reasoned people would actually come and pay to watch terrible weather. It was a brilliant scheme that gained ground over the years up and down the Pacific Coast and became its own tourist industry, maybe because people get bored in winter and discover they feel exhilaratingly alive in the teeth of a raging storm blown in from Alaska—a wild and primordial feeling just when the gray lid of a Northwest winter threatens to sink you.

Tofino is on the receiving end of ten to fifteen serious storms during the winter season. They slam the coast from November through February, with December and January peak times. Add to the mix that you can watch the raw power beside a warm fire in a luxurious setting or don your Gore-Tex and meet the storm head on—you have the best of both worlds.

There are several ferry options to get you to **Vancouver Island** and onto Tofino: BC Ferries, Black Ball Ferry, and the passenger-only *Victoria Clipper* out of Seattle (see Resources, page 223). Once on Vancouver Island you will experience a memorably gorgeous drive from Nanaimo to Tofino. Get your weekend provisions in **Coombs** at the Coombs Old Country Market, which has a wide array of international foods, a bakery, a deli, and goats that graze on the grass roof. Thirteen miles west of Coombs, stop at Cathedral Grove in MacMillan Provincial Park, where you can stretch your legs and walk in the shadows of majestic Douglas fir trees more than 800 years old.

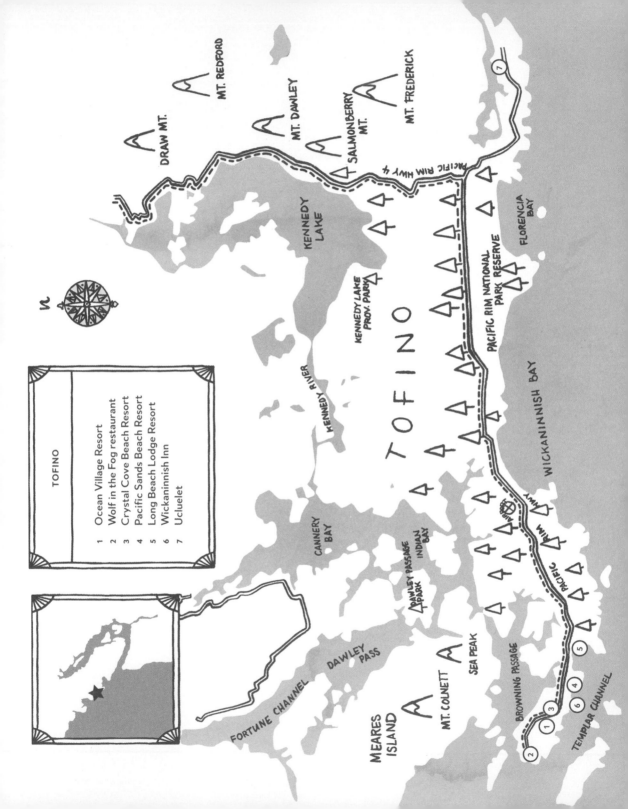

TOFINO

1 Ocean Village Resort
2 Wolf in the Fog restaurant
3 Crystal Cove Beach Resort
4 Pacific Sands Beach Resort
5 Long Beach Lodge Resort
6 Wickaninnish Inn
7 Ucluelet

N

MT. REDFORD
DRAW MT.
MT. DAWLEY
SALMONBERRY MT.
MT. FREDERICK

PACIFIC RIM HWY 4

KENNEDY LAKE

FLORENCIA BAY

KENNEDY LAKE PROV. PARK

PACIFIC RIM NATIONAL PARK RESERVE

KENNEDY RIVER

WICKANINNISH BAY

T O F I N O

CANNERY BAY

DAWLEY PASSAGE PARK

INDIAN BAY

PACIFIC

MEARES ISLAND

MT. COLNETT

SEA PEAK

DAWLEY PASS

FORTUNE CHANNEL

BROWNING PASSAGE

TEMPLAR CHANNEL

1
2
3
4
5
6
7

The drive continues up Sutton Pass and through the Pacific Rim National Park Reserve. Note that mud- and snow-designated tires are required on BC Highway 4 along the Pacific Rim Highway from October 1 through March 31. During your stay in Tofino, make reservations at the Wolf in the Fog restaurant (WolfintheFog.com) and order the delectable potato-crusted oysters or the grilled lamb sausage. The Shelter is another not-to-miss restaurant (ShelterRestaurant.com). Order the Tofino Surf Bowl or indulge in their fresh local seafood.

There is a wide range of accommodation options in Tofino, from swanky to average, with most resorts and lodges offering winter rates. The following are some of my favorites.

Pacific Sands Beach Resort
Located on Cox Bay at the edge of the Pacific Rim National Park Reserve, this lovely resort offers a wide range of accommodations from family-friendly suites with kitchens to lodge rooms and beach houses. PacificSands.com

Ocean Village Resort
These reasonably priced beachfront cabins have an upper and a lower unit and are steps away from MacKenzie Beach. OceanVillageResort.com

Crystal Cove Beach Resort
There are many choices and price ranges at this beautiful resort, from private RV sites to deluxe cabins with private hot tubs. You can also try glamping (short for glamorous camping) and rent a trailer. The resort is situated on MacKenzie Beach. CrystalCove.ca

Long Beach Lodge Resort
Another resort on Cox Bay, this one has an on-site surf school. It has family-friendly self-contained cottages as well as beautiful rooms in the lodge. Be sure to check the specials and deals for the best winter rates. LongBeachLodgeResort.com

WINTER STORM-WATCHING TIPS AND TRICKS

Before going:

- Keep your dates flexible and watch the weather for brewing low-pressure systems. The best weather sites for the Northwest are the National Weather Service (Weather.gov) and Cliff Mass's site (CliffMass.Blogspot.com) for forecasts and analysis.
- Read the tide table (see How to Read a Tide Table, page 8) for your location. Winter storm waves are best at high tide.

If watching from the shore:

- Stay warm! Wear waterproof jackets, waterproof pants, hat, and gloves when out in the storm. The Scandinavians have a saying that there is no such thing as bad weather, only bad gear. Wear the right gear.
- Do not stand on the rocks of a seemingly safe jetty during a storm. Rogue and sneaker waves have claimed many lives.
- Sneaker waves are impossible to predict and can flash up on the beach with deadly force, particularly during storms. Stay aware of the surf, and keep a safe distance between you and the shoreline.
- While hiking on the beach, stay above the tide line.
- Do not turn your back on the surf. In a winter storm, random waves can sweep you off your feet.
- Watch the driftwood logs! They are lethal missiles in the water and can smash into you. Four inches of water can move a 5-ton log with deadly force.
- Stay on land, well away from the presence of rip currents. They rush back out to sea, taking everything with them. Flotsam and foam floating on the water are indications of rip currents.

Wickaninnish Inn
If budget is not an issue, stay at the Wick. It is a luxe lodge with spectacular ocean views, a spa, and a fabulous restaurant to eat at on a stormy day. WickInn.com

More Storm-Watching Sites: Washington

Cape Flattery
Cape Flattery is legendary. It is the northwesternmost point of the contiguous United States and it is isolated, wild in any weather, and breathtaking. In **Neah Bay** stop at the Makah Museum to buy the required recreational permit to park at Cape Flattery. While you are there check out the stunning exhibits and artifacts from Makah culture. Then make your way to the trailhead and hike the 0.75-mile trail that winds through forest to one of the three viewing platforms. You'll feel you are on the prow of a ship overlooking the Pacific as you watch monstrous waves crashing onto the cliffs below. Stay at Hobuck Beach Resort (HobuckBeachResort.com), a short drive away on Hobuck Beach. The beach is stellar, with surfers, paddlers, and beachcombers out between storms.

La Push
Pacific storms pound **La Push** in winter. There is only one place to stay: the Quileute Oceanside Resort (QuileuteOceanside.com), which is owned by the Quileute Tribe. Reserve a deluxe cabin for a front-porch view of the Pacific Ocean, and plan on cooking; there are few restaurants. You are cut off from the outside world here—there is no television, the internet connection is available in the office only, and cell coverage is spotty—but the isolation from technology makes the storm watching a singular and undistracted experience, rare in our socially connected world.

Kalaloch Beach

There are many reasons Kalaloch (pronounced Clay-lock) Beach is considered one of the best places for storm watching in Washington: the direct hit of storms during winter and the outstanding beachcombing, not to mention it is part of the 70 miles of wilderness beach on the Olympic Peninsula. The main place to stay is Kalaloch Lodge (TheKalalochLodge.com), or reserve one of the bluff cabins and plan to make your own meals for your stay.

Mocrocks, Copalis, and Ocean Shores Beaches

Add razor clamming (see page 146) to storm watching, and you have a recipe for adventure. Mocrocks Beach, Copalis Beach, and Ocean Shores are all prime storm-watching and razor-clamming beaches. Watch the storms roll in and dig for the delectable razor clam in your rain gear. Stay at the Iron Springs Resort (IronSpringsResort.com) in one of its charming cabins. It also sometimes offers guided razor-clam digs for newbies.

More Storm-Watching Sites: Oregon

Seaside

Seaside is the family-friendly alternative for storm watching, with a long promenade for walking and biking, and the Seaside Aquarium (SeasideAquarium.com) to explore in between storms. Accommodations are less expensive than in nearby Cannon Beach, and if you stay at Tides by the Sea (TheTidesbytheSea.com), you can watch surfers ride the waves in the cove and return to cozy warmth beside a wood-burning fireplace. Have breakfast at the Firehouse Grill (FirehouseGrill.org, closed Tuesdays and Wednesdays), and on your way out of town, bring an ice-filled cooler for a mandatory stop at the seafood stand Bell Buoy (BellBuoyofSeaside.com) to load up on sweet and meaty Dungeness crab or cleaned and bagged razor clams.

Cannon Beach

It's the beach that draws people here year round. Cinematic Haystack Rock—one of the world's largest volcanic monoliths—rises 235 feet out of the water beside a wide and sandy beach stretching for miles. The Schooner's Cove Inn (SchoonersCove.com) has an oceanfront view and is a short walk away from the bistros, coffeehouses, and galleries of this charming town. Add romance to the teeth of the storm and stay at the luxurious four-star Stephanie Inn (Stephanie-Inn.com): deluxe rooms with spectacular views, a Jacuzzi, and a deck overlooking the ocean. Don't miss breakfast at the Lazy Susan Café (Lazy-Susan-Cafe.com), and order the ginger waffles with fresh pears. For epic, in-your-face storm watching, head a few miles north to Ecola State Park, then return to your warm nest.

Lincoln City

There is a fabulous place in **Lincoln City** perched on a bluff above the ocean, called the Ester Lee (EsterLee.com). Motel is too small a word for the expansive seascape of the Pacific Ocean visible from every window of its rooms and cottages. The views are epic, there are fireplaces in all of the cottages, it is pet-friendly, and best of all, you get a million-dollar view of winter storms for a reasonable rate.

Eat lunch or dinner at Hearth and Table (bit.ly/2upAuI3) in town, where the menu changes daily with whatever fresh and local ingredients are available. Save room for dessert!

Heceta Head

Heceta Head (bit.ly/2qFxndF), between **Florence** and **Yachats** (pronounced "Yah-hots"), is a working lighthouse restored to include a small boutique bed-and-breakfast that offers a dazzling perspective on the Pacific as well as a sumptuous multicourse breakfast. Watch the storms from the wide porch, or get wet and hike the short trail to the lighthouse at night—this is the strongest lighthouse light on the Oregon coast, shooting light 21 miles out to sea.

ROAD TRIP: LIGHTHOUSES ON THE WASHINGTON AND OREGON COASTS

There are many reasons to love a lighthouse: its hold on high ground, the long view of the horizon, the strong light marking the danger to steer from—all metaphors that speak to the human condition. The Washington and Oregon coasts are home to thirty-five lighthouses on the edge of the sea, and a leisurely road trip is the perfect way to scout them out. This itinerary includes three lighthouses you can stay in overnight, and one you can work in for a week doing lighthouse-keeper duties. Consider breaking up the trip if it is too long to do in one chunk.

New Dungeness Lighthouse

Begin your trip here, near **Sequim**, Washington, with the only long hike on the itinerary, worth every step of the way. The trailhead is located in the Dungeness National Wildlife Refuge, where there is a $3 entrance fee for up to four people. The windswept and stunning 11-mile round-trip to the lighthouse is an all-day affair; plan to hike at low tide for easier walking, pack a picnic, and bring rain gear. Dungeness Spit, where the lighthouse is located, juts out into the Strait of Juan de Fuca and grows 15 inches every year from river sediment and eroding bluffs. The working lighthouse, constructed in 1857 near the end of the spit, now sits over a half mile from the tip. Do you want more? New Dungeness has a program where you can work for a week performing the regular duties of a lighthouse keeper: bit.ly/1RVG6jL. One of the jobs of the resident lighthouse keeper is to give tours; knock on the door and ask for one.

After the hike, head back across the Hood Canal Bridge to the lighthouse at Point No Point in **Hansville**, about an hour-and-a-half drive. Stop at Albertsons grocery store (bit.ly/2tqKwMm) at the corner of Hansville Road NE and State Route 104 to pick up breakfast supplies for the morning.

Point No Point Lighthouse

Point No Point is the oldest lighthouse on Puget Sound (New Dungeness, although older, is on the Strait of Juan de Fuca) and has been in continuous operation since it was completed in 1879. Today it is leased from the US Coast Guard by Kitsap County Parks and Recreation, which set up half of the historic lighthouse keepers' duplex as a vacation rental

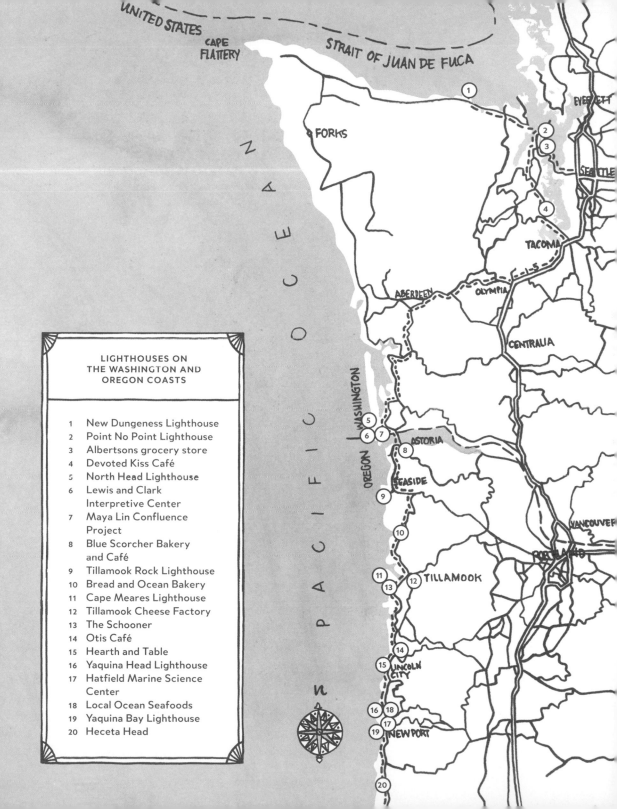

LIGHTHOUSES ON
THE WASHINGTON AND
OREGON COASTS

1   New Dungeness Lighthouse
2   Point No Point Lighthouse
3   Albertsons grocery store
4   Devoted Kiss Café
5   North Head Lighthouse
6   Lewis and Clark
    Interpretive Center
7   Maya Lin Confluence
    Project
8   Blue Scorcher Bakery
    and Café
9   Tillamook Rock Lighthouse
10 Bread and Ocean Bakery
11 Cape Meares Lighthouse
12 Tillamook Cheese Factory
13 The Schooner
14 Otis Café
15 Hearth and Table
16 Yaquina Head Lighthouse
17 Hatfield Marine Science
    Center
18 Local Ocean Seafoods
19 Yaquina Bay Lighthouse
20 Heceta Head

(bit.ly/29497LN), and the other half to house the US Lighthouse Society executive offices. To set up a tour of the lighthouse during the winter, email docents@pnplighthouse.com.

In the morning put on your coat, take your coffee to the porch, and drink in the spectacular view. Spend the morning beachcombing, and if you haven't set up a tour of the lighthouse for later in the day, pack up and head south to your next lighthouse accommodation: North Head Lighthouse at Cape Disappointment State Park, an approximately 4-hour drive without stops, but add some time and stop for lunch in **Gig Harbor** at Devoted Kiss Café (DevotedKissCafe.com), which overlooks the harbor, and order the divine smoked-salmon benedict.

North Head Lighthouse

What's known as the "Graveyard of the Pacific" includes a treacherous bar created where the mighty Columbia River joins the Pacific Ocean, which has caused thousands of devastating shipwrecks over the centuries. Two lighthouses were built here to mark the danger. The first one, built in 1856, was the Cape Disappointment Lighthouse, but mariners coming from the north protested that the light was not visible until vessels ran aground. North Head was built 2 miles away and put into service in 1898 to expand navigational aid. North Head is one of the windiest locations on the Washington coast (good for storm watching!) and an exhilarating place to explore. Stay for 2 nights to take advantage of the miles of trails and beaches in the park and to explore nearby Astoria. Visit bit.ly/2rZ7f1h to make reservations.

A short walk from the North Head parking lot takes you to the cliff where this striking structure holds its stony perch. You will need a Discover Pass (DiscoverPass.wa.gov) to park here (if you live in Washington, you can buy one when you renew your vehicle tabs; you will use the pass around the state for parking at state parks). For a small fee you can climb the steps to the top of the lighthouse and gaze out to the sweeping vista. North Head's first lens was a first-order Fresnel lens (see Lighthouse Terms, opposite page) that now resides in the Lewis and Clark Interpretive Center, which also provides a historical overview of Lewis and Clark's epic journey to the Pacific Ocean. Fresnel lenses have their own strange beauty with glass panels and prisms.

LIGHTHOUSE TERMS

Most specialized occupations have unique words that reflect their realm, and lighthouses are no exception. The following terms are a useful word map of this fascinating world.

- **ARC OF VISIBILITY:** The portion of the horizon that a lighted aid (from a lighthouse, for example) is visible from the sea.
- **DAYMARK:** The painted pattern and color scheme unique to each lighthouse.
- **FRESNEL LENS:** A compact lens developed by French physicist Augustin-Jean Fresnel in 1822 that revolutionized the lights of lighthouses. A Fresnel lens increases the brightness and the reach of the light and decreases the mass and volume of material needed to manufacture it. Fresnel lenses are ranked in six refracting orders based on their length and focal width. A first-order light is the largest and brightest, and a sixth-order light the smallest.
- **LANTERN ROOM:** The glassed-in housing at the top of a lighthouse where the light operates.
- **LIGHT LIST:** All ships have a book called a "light list" that the navigator refers to; it gives detailed information on navigational aids, including each lighthouse's daymark to identify it while navigating by day and its unique light signature seen at night.
- **LIGHT SIGNATURE:** The sequence of light flashes and pauses, unique to each lighthouse so navigators can identify it at night.
- **NAUTICAL MILE:** Picture this: If you were to cut the earth in half at the equator, you could lift it up and see the equator as a circle. Divide that circle into 360 degrees, then divide a single degree into 60 minutes. Each one of those minutes is a nautical mile. Nautical miles are used globally for air and sea travel primarily because there are no mile markers at sea, and latitude is easily measured. The power of a lighthouse light is typically measured in nautical miles.
- **SOUND SIGNAL:** A transmission of sound used to warn mariners of hazardous conditions when it is foggy and the light cannot be seen.
- **WATCH ROOM:** A windowed room typically right under the lantern room, where a lighthouse keeper could watch weather and water conditions during a storm.
- **WICKIE:** Slang for lighthouse keeper, named for the task of trimming the wicks of lamps.

There are also many opportunities for outdoor activities during your stay at North Head Lighthouse. Hike the beaches, including Waikiki, where a summer concert series is held (see page 64). At Waikiki check out the Maya Lin Confluence Project, commemorating Lewis and Clark's journey, or hike the multiple trails through canopies of trees.

On your way out of town toward Heceta Head, your next lighthouse accommodation, plan on breakfast in **Astoria** at the Blue Scorcher Bakery and Café (BlueScorcher.coop). If you drive without stopping, Heceta Head is close to a 4.5-hour drive away, but there are stops ahead of you! First up, Ecola State Park for a view of Tillamook Rock Lighthouse.

Tillamook Rock Lighthouse

The privately owned and decommissioned Tillamook Rock Lighthouse could be the unluckiest lighthouse on the Pacific. It was built in 1880 on a mere rock off the coast at much expense and with many setbacks and sacrifices. Its precarious perch was continuously battered by waves and violent storms that regularly caused extensive damage. It was a "stag light"—only men tended the light, as it was considered too dangerous for women and families—and it quickly became known as "Terrible Tilly" for the harrowing weather and miserable work conditions. The US Coast Guard finally gave up, decommissioned Terrible Tilly in 1957, and sold it. It changed hands and was eventually bought by a group of investors who made it into the Eternity at Sea Columbarium for holding cremated remains, but the license was revoked when it was revealed that there was inaccurate record keeping and improper storage of the urns. For more information visit bit.ly/1e19o9Y.

The next stop is Bread and Ocean Bakery (bit.ly/2uwRtf7), a bakery and deli in **Manzanita**, for lunch and snacks for the road. Then, as you drive into **Tillamook**, make a short detour to the Tillamook Cheese Factory's visitor center (Tillamook.com) and watch the classic cheese being made. Plan to arrive at Heceta Head Lighthouse before dark if possible to find the somewhat hidden entrance to the lighthouse, so carry on. The drive is approximately 2.5 hours from Tillamook.

Heceta Head Lighthouse

The light of Heceta (pronounced "Ha-see-ta") Head Lighthouse, the strongest on the Oregon coast, blazes out into the Pacific Ocean for 21 miles. Built on a cliff with a trail to the beach, this splendid lighthouse is one of the most photographed on the West Coast. It was constructed in 1892 and is now on the National Register of Historic Places. Base yourself at the lighthouse's bed-and-breakfast (bit.ly/2qFFuqJ) for 2 nights for more exploring of Yaquina Bay, Yaquina Head, and Cape Meares Lighthouses. Be sure to hike from the keeper's house, where you stay, to the lighthouse at night for an unforgettable experience. Prepare yourself for a sumptuous multi-course gourmet breakfast in the morning, then head north to Yaquina Bay Lighthouse, a 45-minute drive.

Yaquina Bay Lighthouse

Yaquina (pronounced "Ya-kwin-ah") Bay Lighthouse (bit.ly/2uq8Z1g) had a brief, inglorious working life. Built in 1871 and declared too squat and too short, it was decommissioned just 3 years later because big sister Yaquina Head Lighthouse, built a few miles away, was taller, brighter, and quite simply outshone it. Today the Oregon Parks and Recreation Department has restored the Yaquina Bay Lighthouse to working order so it, too, can help boaters navigate. The lighthouse is open to the public every day except holidays. November through February the lighthouse is closed on Mondays and Tuesdays.

Yaquina Head Lighthouse

This is the tallest and perhaps the most picturesque lighthouse in Oregon. Yaquina Head Lighthouse (on.doi.gov/2hCoU6R) continues to beam the original 1868 Fresnel lens 19 miles out to sea. February through June, tours are offered depending on weather conditions and available staff. Call ahead (541-574-3100) for the current schedule. July through September, tours are offered daily. Go down to Cobble Beach, below the lighthouse, composed of millions of round basalt rocks that sound like applause when the waves roll in.

Next, head 4 miles south to **Newport** for the attractions: the Oregon Coast Aquarium (Aquarium.org) for a walk under a shark tank; Hatfield Marine Science Center (hmsc.OregonState.edu), a five-star playground of science and wonder, for an up-close and personal view of a giant Pacific

octopus (and do not miss the sand table); and a must-stop at Local Ocean Seafoods (LocalOcean.net) for the best seafood you will find anywhere.

The next morning, turn north for the final lighthouse on the trip, Cape Meares, about a 3-hour drive from Heceta Head. You have a choice for lunch: Hearth and Table in **Lincoln City**, or a slight detour east on State Route 18 near Lincoln City to **Otis**, for Otis Café's (OtisCafe.com) world-renowned German potatoes: crispy hash browns topped with green onions and white cheddar cheese. Waddle on! Still hungry? Stop in **Netarts** at the Schooner (TheSchooner.net) for oysters. You will burn those calories at Cape Meares Lighthouse.

Cape Meares Lighthouse

The lighthouse viewpoint is located 10 miles west of Tillamook on a headland 200 feet above the ocean. It is a short hike from the Cape Meares Light trailhead parking lot to the decommissioned lighthouse, and within Cape Meares Lighthouse and Wildlife Refuge there is plenty to do: The trailhead to Oregon's largest living Sitka spruce, estimated to be between 750 and 800 years old, is near the park entrance. There is also the Octopus Tree to hike to—another massive Sitka spruce with heavy branches sprouting horizontally like tentacles. Tribal descendants say it was cultivated as a ceremonial site to hold cedar canoes. The Octopus Tree is recognized today as one of many Native ceremonial trees, living icons of tribal culture. bit.ly/2u4M4Jt

BEST WINTER BEACH HIKES

Why hike in winter? We need the outdoors most during the long, dull skies of the season. Prepare for any weather and bring out the rain gear. Here is a list of shore hikes that will elevate the grayest of days.

British Columbia

- **VANCOUVER ISLAND**: Long Beach near Tofino
- **VANCOUVER**: Foreshore Trail at Pacific Spirit Regional Park

Washington

- **BELLINGHAM**: Padilla Bay Shore Trail
- **WHIDBEY ISLAND**: Double Bluff State Park beach (dogs are allowed to be off leash)
- **PORT TOWNSEND**: Point Wilson Lighthouse at Fort Worden State Park
- **SEQUIM**: Dungeness Spit (check tide tables to walk at low tide)
- **SEATTLE**: Discovery Park Loop Trail; Lincoln Park trails
- **TACOMA**: Owen Beach
- **WASHINGTON COAST**: Kalaloch Beach; Discovery Trail (on the Long Beach Peninsula); Cape Disappointment Lighthouse Loop Trail

Oregon

- **OREGON COAST**: Ecola Point to Indian Beach (at Ecola State Park); Cape Trail (at Cape Lookout State Park)

MICRO-ADVENTURE: HIKE A SECRET STATE PARK

Explore a secret park boasting one of the longest undeveloped shore-lines in the Puget Sound area. Miller Peninsula, about 13 miles southeast of **Sequim**, Washington, has a 19-mile trail network and miles of empty beach with expansive views of the Strait of Juan de Fuca. Washington State Parks acquired the property in the 1990s but lacked the funds to develop an infrastructure, leaving it gloriously unknown and empty. This is a great park for dogs. Exploring the trails on Miller Peninsula is a good opportunity to brush up on your navigation skills; it's easy to get lost. bit.ly/2rKeEBG

Catch it, Cook it, Eat it

CRAB

Eating a fresh Dungeness crab is pure bliss—it is sweet and meaty, tasting of the sea and everything Northwest. It's no wonder that its scientific name, *Metacarcinus magister*, means "master crab." It is the taste master of all crab, and it is easy to catch them yourself during open crab-fishing season. In the Puget Sound area, Washington Department of Fish and Wildlife, along with Native treaty tribes, determines the recreational openings to maintain a sustainable fishery, and the season usually begins in early summer and some years runs into winter.

Tips and Tricks
- Crabbing is easiest in summer, but winter is when these delectable crustaceans are in peak numbers in grocery stores, if your crab pots haul up empty. Consider this a late-spring fishery as well.
- Canada and each state have different restrictions. Check your local fishing regulations before throwing a crab trap (see Resources, page 223).
- You may also catch red rock crab in your traps. They are smaller than a Dungeness and also good eating but do not have the plentiful meat and delicious flavor of a Dungeness. They can be identified by the black tips at the ends of their claws.

Where to Go
For more localized information, ask experienced crabbers where they like to go, but here are a few places to get you started.

British Columbia
VANCOUVER
- **WEST VANCOUVER:** Ambleside Park
- **BELCARRA:** Belcarra Regional Park

VANCOUVER ISLAND
- **NANAIMO:** Fishing and Walking Pier at Nanaimo Harbor
- **SIDNEY:** Port Sidney Marina dock
- **SOOKE:** Sooke Rotary Pier

Washington
NORTH PUGET SOUND
- **BAYVIEW:** Padilla Bay
- **CAMANO ISLAND:** Camano Island State Park
- **WHIDBEY ISLAND:** Skagit Bay

CENTRAL PUGET SOUND
- **EDMONDS:** Browns Bay
- **SEATTLE:** Elliott Bay off Alki Point, Shilshole Bay

SOUTH PUGET SOUND
- **GIG HARBOR:** Carr Inlet
- **DES MOINES:** Poverty Bay
- **OLYMPIA:** Nisqually Reach

Oregon
- **ROCKAWAY BEACH:** Kelly's Brighton Marina
- **LINCOLN CITY:** Siletz Moorage
- **NEWPORT:** Embarcadero Resort Hotel and Marina

Equipment
- **SHELLFISH LICENSE** with crab endorsement (see Resources, page 223)
- **CRAB TRAP**—the old guard holds that square traps catch more crab than round ones
- **4- TO 7-POUND LEAD BAR** to weight the trap in the water so it won't travel with the current
- **BAIT BOX**—the round plastic ones with a screw top are easiest to refill, and the crab can't plunder the bait like they can with the mesh type
- **BAIT**—your best bet is to use a chicken or turkey drumstick; next in line: a rockfish, salmon carcass, or herring
- **50 TO 100 FEET OF LEADED LINE** (the length will depend on the depth of the water where you crab)
- **RED-AND-WHITE BUOY** with your name and phone number written on it, if you are crabbing by boat
- **RUBBER GLOVES,** for protecting your hands

CRABBING AT KELLY'S BRIGHTON MARINA

I don't know any place quite like Kelly's Brighton Marina (Kellys BrightonMarina.com) in **Rockaway Beach**. It is a retreat for the urbanites who want to wear a fisherman knit sweater and rubber boots, head out onto a lovely bay to go crabbing, then have their crab cooked while drinking beer beside an outdoor fire and take goofy photos of friends through wooden cutouts of pirates and mermaids. Kelly's Brighton Marina is a classic Northwest experience not to be missed.

New to crabbing? It offers boats to rent by the hour, complete with life jackets, a crab pot, and bait (shellfish licenses can be purchased on-site), and the staff is happy to show you how to do it all before heading out. Motor back and Kelly's will then cook the crab you caught and serve it with one of a good variety of beers to choose from. Or you can simply order crab someone else has caught and sit at the picnic table and pick the sweet meat from the shell.

Make reservations to stay in a yurt at Nehalem Bay State Park to extend the weekend. The park includes a portion of the dramatic Oregon Coast Trail (bit.ly/2smG3ux) that runs along the coast here. If you are sky-hopping by private plane, there is an airstrip at the park to land at, and you can walk to the yurt.

- **CRAB CALIPER**, for measuring the carapace of the male crab for size limitations (it is illegal to harvest females)
- **COOLER** or 5-gallon bucket with ice, for storing the crab
- **OLD TOWEL**

Techniques

The location for your trap is important. Crab tend to settle in the channels formed by tides and river flow. Dungies love sandy bottoms, and docks are often good places to throw your pot. If you have access to a boat, even better; you will be able to widen the range. Leave the traps in the water anywhere from 30 minutes to several hours.

To set up your trap, zip-tie the filled bait box inside the trap at the top, place the weight inside the trap, and tie the leaded line on top. If you are crabbing by boat, secure the buoy at the end of the line.

By Pier or Dock

This is the easiest crabbing method. Fill the bait box with bait. Drop the pot in the water until it hits the bottom, then fasten the end of the line to a railing or someplace secure. Check the tides; the best time to catch crab from a dock or pier is when the tide is coming in, pulling them in toward shore.

By Boat, Kayak, or SUP

Check the nautical chart for the area you plan to drop the trap. The depth is important. If you tie on a 50-foot line and drop the pot in 75 feet of water, you'll lose everything. Drop the baited trap and note the GPS coordinates if you plan on leaving the site.

CRAB POT SETUP

From the Shore
Wading from shore can be effective and puts you in the trenches with the crab. You will need waders, a dip net, and a minus tide (see How to Read a Tide Table, page 8) for this technique. In the winter most minus tides are at night. Go with a partner who can hold a light or a lantern so you can see the crab and scoop them up with your net.

Pulling Crab from the Pot
Retrieving crab from the traps is an art. They can grip the trap bars with their claws, pinch your hands, and scrabble menacingly around. Put on rubber gloves and pick them up by the back legs so they can't pinch you. Turn them over to determine if they are male or female. Females have a broader abdominal flap, or apron, than males, and are illegal to keep. Use the caliper to measure the carapace to see if the male is large enough to keep, or if measuring by hand, measure in a straight line across the widest part of the shell. Note that British Columbia's Dungeness crab must measure 6.5 inches in order to harvest. In Washington they must measure 6.25 inches, and in Oregon, 5.75 inches.

FEMALE CRAB

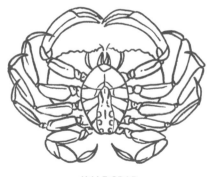

MALE CRAB

How to Store and Clean a Crab

Keep the crab damp and cool once out of the water. Place them in a cooler or 5-gallon bucket, cover them with a towel dipped in seawater, and place ice on top of the towel. Do not store them in a covered cooler or in freshwater or they will suffocate. Crab can live up to 24 hours refrigerated, but it is important to cook them as soon as possible after catching.

The easiest way to clean a crab is to steam it first. Steaming is favored over immersing it in boiling water to keep the meat sweeter and less waterlogged.

Tamale steamers (the 15.5-quart size) are an excellent choice for steaming crab and are inexpensive. If you don't have a steamer large enough, improvise with a long piece of aluminum foil rolled loosely into a 1-inch-thick snake. Shape it into a spiral in the bottom of a large pot with a lid. Add 1 inch of water to the pot and bring to a boil over high heat. Using tongs, pick the crab up from behind and place it into the pot. Steam one crab at a time. Cover with a lid, reduce the heat to medium, and steam for 7 to 8 minutes per pound—10 to 15 minutes for an average-size crab. When done, using tongs, remove the crab and rinse it with cold water.

Now you are ready for cleaning: Turn the crab over and remove the abdomen, or apron (see Figure 1). Remove the outer shell by sticking your thumb into the hole left by the removal of the apron and lift up (see Figure 2). Remove the white leaflike gills from both sides of the body. Break off the two sides of the mandibles (the mouth of the crab). Rinse off all the viscera. Turn the crab upside down and break it in half along the middle of the back with a set of claws on each half. Use a sharp knife to cut the crab into smaller pieces between the legs, leaving a nice chunk of body meat on the end. Place the cooked crab pieces in a large ziplock bag, seal, and refrigerate until ready to eat. They will keep 3 to 5 days.

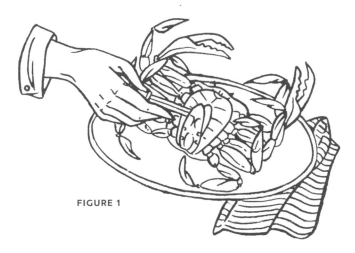

FIGURE 1

FIGURE 2

CITIZEN SCIENCE: WATCH FOR INVASIVE EUROPEAN GREEN CRAB

There is a small but growing population in the Salish Sea of European green crab, considered one of the world's worst invasive species. This aggressive crab voraciously eats shellfish and native shore crab, destroys eelgrass beds, and crowds out other wildlife in the marine ecosystem. These crab can decimate a fragile ecosystem if they are left unchecked. They are found in a wide range of habitats, including rocky beaches and shores, sand flats, and tidal marshes, and sometimes will appear in crab pots. The carapace is broader than it is long with the crab rarely growing over 4 inches in length. They are identified not by their green color, which varies, but by five toothlike spines on each side of the shell. Report a European green crab sighting by following these steps:

- Identify the crab using bit.ly/2qLR0jx.
- Take several photos from different angles and with some indicator of scale.
- In British Columbia, catch it and freeze it. Note the location and contact Fisheries and Oceans Canada (bit.ly/2vfU5vB).
- In Washington, do not remove it! It is illegal to possess a green crab without a special permit. Place it back where you found it. Email your photos to crabteam@uw.edu. The University of Washington research team will quickly follow up if it is a green crab and search for more where you discovered it.
- In Oregon, take three digital photos and report it to the invasive species hotline: bit.ly/2tsjiog.

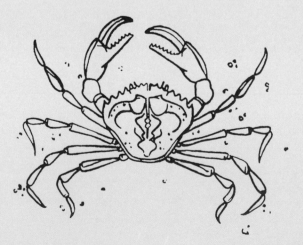

Holiday Dinner Crab Feast

MAKES 6 SERVINGS

Featuring crab for the holiday dinner is a tradition in our house. We spread the big table with butcher paper, tape it securely in place, and add felt-tip markers for the kids to decorate the place settings. A crab feast is a gloriously informal meal that leaves the cook relaxed and everyone happy to eat with their fingers as time disappears in conversation and laughter.

INGREDIENTS:

6 crab

1 cup Chili Butter Dipping
   Sauce (recipe follows)
   or melted butter

Green salad and crusty
   bread, for serving

Steam and clean the crab as described on page 142. Reheat refrigerated crab by placing an inch or two of water in a tamale steamer. Bring the water to a boil over high heat, add the crab pieces to the steamer basket, cover with the lid, and steam for about 5 minutes, or until you smell them cooking.

Put small bowls of the dipping sauce on the table.

Add a big green salad with your favorite homemade vinaigrette—a lovely, pungent counterpoint to the crab—and a loaf of crusty bread (and a rich dessert!), and you are set.

Use the small, sharp ends of the crab claws to pick out the meat after cracking the claws with nutcrackers.

Put empty shells in big bowls on the table to keep them separate.

When finished, roll up the butcher-paper tablecloth and throw it away, unless you want to save some of the table decorations and tape them on the refrigerator.

Chili Butter Dipping Sauce

MAKES ½ CUP

Make this chili butter for those who like the heat. (Serve plain melted butter for the purists.) You can substitute an aji rojo or red Thai chili pepper for the cayenne.

INGREDIENTS:

½ cup (1 stick) unsalted butter

2 garlic cloves, minced

1 fresh cayenne pepper, minced

2 tablespoons fresh chives, minced, for serving

In a heavy saucepan over medium-low heat, melt the butter. Add the garlic and cayenne, and simmer for about 2 minutes, then remove from the heat and allow to sit for 1 hour. To serve, warm the chili butter over medium-low heat or in the microwave for 10 seconds, and sprinkle with chives.

RAZOR CLAMS

Just when the gray skies lock down the Pacific Northwest and most people head indoors, there is another world of outdoor enthusiasts and clam lovers who welcome winter. It is the season of razor clams. Razor clams are considered the delicious big boys of the Northwest clam world, and digging for them takes a keen eye, a tolerance for cold weather, and a love for being outdoors by the shore. Don't miss out on this classic Northwest dig up and down the Pacific Coast. If the low tide opening is at night, which it often is, seize the opportunity for a nighttime beach adventure. Always call the hotline for beach closures due to marine toxins before digging. British Columbia: 1-866-431-3474. Washington: 1-800-562-5632. Oregon: 1-800-448-2474.

Where to Go

British Columbia
- Tofino's Long Beach

Washington
- Long Beach
- Twin Harbors Beach
- Copalis Beach
- Mocrocks Beach

Oregon
- Fort Stevens State Park Beach
- Sunset Beach
- Del Rey Beach
- Gearhart Beach
- Seaside Beach

Equipment
- Shellfish license (see Resources, page 223)
- Good rain gear, Gore-Tex waders if you have them, and rubber boots
- Clam shovel or razor clam gun (both available at most tackle and outdoor stores)
- Bucket, for putting the clams in (all diggers must have their own buckets)
- Flashlight or lantern, for night digs

Technique
Walk near the tide line at low tide and look for a show in the wet sand. A show is a small hole left when the clam withdraws its neck and dives down into the sand. There are three types of show: a dimple, a small, circular depression in the sand; a keyhole, a very distinct hole usually in drier sand; and a doughnut, a hole with raised sides around it. Razor clams are fast and can dig about 1 foot in 30 seconds. Most clams lie between 6 and 24 inches deep. If you are using a clam gun (basically a piece of pipe with handles and an air hole), turn to face the ocean and place the tube of the gun in the center over the show. Make sure the air hole on the handle is free, then plunge the gun straight down, working the pipe a little from side to side to dig deep. Place your thumb over the air hole on the handle to seal it and lift the tube, rocking it slightly back and forth. Use your legs to lift! Wet sand is heavy and you will be doing this at least fifteen times. Remove your thumb from the air hole and the sand will release. Check the pile of sand for a clam.

CLAM GUN

Using a clam shovel requires a slightly different technique. Place the shovel blade seaward about 6 inches from the show with the handle angled toward land. Use your body weight to push the shovel blade straight into the sand, keeping the blade as vertical as possible so you don't smash into the clam, and drop to one knee. Keep one hand low on the handle, close to the blade, and the other near the top of the handle. Pull the handle back so the sand cracks. Remove the sand to get to the clam by diagonally and gently scraping the shovel across the cracked sand until the clam appears. Use your hands to grab it. Put your clam in the empty bucket and refill the hole.

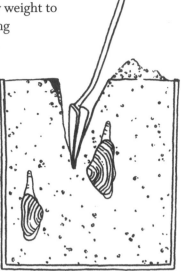

CLAM SHOVEL TECHNIQUE

TYPES OF RAZOR CLAM SHOWS

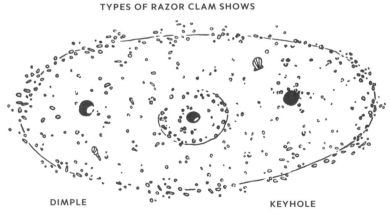

DIMPLE

DOUGHNUT

KEYHOLE

How to Clean a Razor Clam

When you are finished digging for the clams, return to your accommodations and clean them as soon as possible. This won't happen on the beach; you need running water and a way to heat it. The first time you clean one, it can be confusing. There are many body parts, layers, and steps, but clean one clam and you will have it down. Begin by rinsing the sand from the clams, then place them in a large pot. Pour boiling water into the pan to cover the clams, wait about 10 seconds, and the clams will pop open. Immediately place them in cold water. The clam meat is easily removed without cutting.

Using scissors, snip off the dark tip of the siphon, then open the body with scissors, cutting from the base of the foot to the tip of the siphon along the part that looks like a zipper. There is another layer to cut open under this; rinse it well. Snip off the two gills and the mouth parts. The digger part, or foot, is a separate and edible part of the clam. Snip the stomach off. There is a clear rod in the foot that releases enzymes to help digest food; discard it. Slit the foot so it lies flat and remove the small intestine. Rinse everything of the dark viscera, and you are ready to cook it.

The best way to learn how to clean razor clams is to watch a YouTube video like this one: bit.ly/2rt983I.

Tips and Tricks

- The best time to dig is 2 hours before the low tide.
- You must keep the first fifteen clams you find, no matter what size they are. A clam with a broken neck or a cracked shell will die, and placing it back in the sand is illegal.
- Some diggers stomp around in the sand near the waterline to get the clams to leave their show, signaling where to dig.
- A general rule of thumb is the bigger the hole, the bigger the clam.
- Dig fast! Razor clams are quick and efficient divers in wet sand.
- If you are new to razor-clam digging, start with a clam gun over a shovel. It is an easier technique.
- Clean the clams as soon as possible after digging, or place on ice, cover with a damp towel, and refrigerate for up to 4 days. Clams of any kind that do not open when cooked should not be eaten.

Pan-Seared Razor Clams with Fennel

MAKES 4 SERVINGS

The simpler the preparation of these delicious clams, the better—and pan searing is the best. If you overcook them, they will be tough; undercook, and the texture is rubbery. Serve with a salad and a baguette split in half, rubbed with olive oil, and grilled.

INGREDIENTS:

7 tablespoons salted butter

2 tablespoons minced fresh fennel bulb

Juice of 1 lemon

2 tablespoons extra-virgin olive oil, plus more as needed

20 razor clams, cleaned and flattened

Chopped fennel greens, for garnish

Preheat the oven to 250 degrees F.

In a small, heavy-bottomed saucepan over low heat, melt the butter. Add the fennel and cook, stirring occasionally, until the butter takes on a golden-brown cast and the fennel is slightly caramelized. Remove the pan from the heat, and stir in the lemon juice. Set aside.

Preheat a cast-iron skillet over medium-high heat. When a drop of water sizzles in the pan, add the oil and swirl it around. Place a few of the clam steaks in the pan and cook until browned, about 2 minutes. Flip and cook the other side until browned, another 2 minutes.

Place the clam steaks on an ovenproof plate, and place in the warm oven. Fry up the rest of the clams, adding more olive oil as needed. Meanwhile, rewarm the fennel butter over low heat. Transfer all the clams to a serving platter and pour the butter over them. For a finishing touch, sprinkle the fennel greens over everything.

Beach Projects

GOLD-PAINTED SEASHELL ORNAMENTS

It is the simplest projects that are the most successful with kids, and this one will bring seashore memories to the holiday season, whether on your tree or tucked into evergreen branches on the holiday table. Gathering the shells at the beach is the best part.

WHAT YOU WILL NEED:
Sheets of newspaper
Seashells
Gold spray paint
Gold cord, for hanging
  the ornament
Hot-glue gun

Spread the newspaper in a well-ventilated area. Lay the shells on the paper. Let the kids do the spray-painting themselves. Allow the shells to dry, turn them over, and spray-paint the other side. When the paint is dry, use the hot-glue gun to glue both ends of the cord to the inside of the shell, creating a loop.

NOTE: Anything spray-painted gold becomes a treasure to young children! Try painting rocks, shells, and driftwood sticks to turn them into pirate bounty and magic wands.

SEA-GLASS VOTIVE

Nothing is easier than this luminous candleholder to show off sea-glass treasures. It makes a uniquely Northwest gift.

WHAT YOU WILL NEED:
Sea glass
2 glass containers, one
  small enough to fit into
  the other with a half
  inch to spare
Votive candle

Place the smaller glass container into the larger one. Insert the sea glass into the space between the jars one piece at a time, layer by layer, turning the jar as you fill it to keep it centered and working from bottom to top. Place the candle inside the smaller jar.

BEST BEACHES TO FIND SEA GLASS

After a winter storm or tidal surge is an excellent time to beachcomb for glass: you can hit the jackpot on a stretch of beach that had little to find before a storm. Here are several places where the pickings are good:

Vancouver Island, British Columbia
- Port Renfrew: Botanical Beach
- Sidney: Tulista Park Beach
- Tofino: Long Beach, Qualicum Beach

Vancouver, British Columbia
- Vancouver: Kitsilano Beach
- White Rock: White Rock Beach

Washington
- Anacortes: Rosario Beach
- Orcas Island: Eastsound Beach and Crescent Beach
- Port Angeles: Ediz Hook
- Port Orchard: the beach at Southworth
- Port Townsend: Glass Beach
- Seattle: Golden Gardens Park and Alki Beach Park
- Whidbey Island: West Beach (at Deception Pass Park) and Penn Cove

Oregon Coast
- Cannon Beach: Haystack Rock
- Lincoln City: Lincoln Beach
- Newport: Otter Rock
- Oceanside: Oceanside Beach State Recreation Site

BEACHSIDE SHELTER HOT DOG ROAST

*Shake it up! Roast hot dogs over an open fire on a winter day when cabin fever
has set in. State parks all over the Northwest have fireplaces located in shelters;
you can pack up the supplies (don't forget the s'mores) and spend the afternoon
in your warm rain gear, roasting the dogs and walking the beach afterward.
Make sure to check that there is not a burn ban and that the shelter is not
reserved. The key is to make it easy; if you can't find a local fireplace and shelter,
opt for the fire rings. Almost all state parks have them.*

WHAT YOU WILL NEED:
Wood
Fire-starting supplies
Hot dogs
Buns
Condiments

Walk the beach to find the perfect roasting stick. Using the wood and
fire-starting supplies, get a fire going. Skewer the hot dogs on the stick you
found, roast them over the fire, and put them in the buns. Top with the
condiments and enjoy!

On the Water

SCUBA DIVING

There is a world below the surface of Puget Sound teeming with sea life. Scuba divers come from all over the globe to encounter the extraordinary giant Pacific octopus and the wolf eel with a face only a mother could love. There are over seventy-five shore-based dive sites within an hour of Seattle, and with them a wide variety of underwater attractions—from shipwrecks to luminous gardens of anemones. For divers in British Columbia, here is a link to ten great dive sites: bit.ly/2s88cku.

Winter is a popular time to scuba dive because there are fewer algae and plankton blooms that reduce visibility. Dry suits make it all possible, keeping you warm even in frigid water.

The best and only place to start if you are new to scuba diving is a dive class. There are dozens of excellent dive centers up and down the Pacific Northwest coast. Scuba diving on the Oregon coast and jetties is tricky, however, and coastal dives are generally for more experienced divers.

Here are some dive shops where you can learn not only how to dive, but also the best places to do it.

British Columbia
- **HORSESHOE BAY**: Sea Dragon Charters (bit.ly/2u5beaI)
- **NORTH VANCOUVER**: Sea to Sky Scuba (SeatoSkyScuba.com)
- **VANCOUVER**: Diving Locker (DivingLocker.ca), Rowands Reef Scuba Shop (RowandsReef.com)
- **BURNABY**: Ocean Quest Dive Centre (DiveOceanQuest.com)
- **VICTORIA**: Frank Whites Dive Store (FrankWhites.com)

Washington

- **BELLINGHAM:** Gone Diving (GoneDiving.org), Washington Divers (WashingtonDivers.net)
- **ANACORTES:** Anacortes Diving and Supply (AnacortesDiving.com)
- **PORT TOWNSEND:** Octopus Gardens (OctopusGardensDiving.com)
- **WHIDBEY ISLAND:** Whidbey Island Dive Center (WhidbeyDive.com)
- **LYNNWOOD:** Lighthouse Diving Center (LighthouseDiving.com)
- **EDMONDS:** Underwater Sports (UnderwaterSports.com)
- **BAINBRIDGE ISLAND:** Exotic Aquatics Scuba and Kayaking (ExoticAquaticsScuba.com)
- **SEATTLE:** Seattle Scuba (SeattleScuba.com), Underwater Sports (UnderwaterSports.com), Seattle Dive Tours (SeattleDiveTours.com)
- **BELLEVUE:** Silent World Diving Systems (Silent-World.com)
- **TACOMA:** Tacoma Scuba (TacomaScuba.com)
- **OLYMPIA:** Underwater Sports (UnderwaterSports.com)
- **VANCOUVER:** Seven Seas Scuba (SevenSeasScuba.com)

Celebrations & Nature

WINTER SOLSTICE BONFIRE

The winter solstice has been symbolic to the human race for centuries. It is the shortest day and the longest night of the year and marks the return of the sun—promising, as dark and dim as the days are, that the light will return. In astronomical terms the solstice is when the sun is positioned at its lowest point in the sky, December 21 or 22, and the highest, around June 21.

Chase away the darkness with a bonfire, the symbolic guide to the other side of winter, and add the glow of these tiny wish boats (see next page) for a night to remember.

Tips and Tricks
- Check there is no burn ban in effect:
  - **BRITISH COLUMBIA:** bit.ly/28YQDMU
  - **PUGET SOUND:** bit.ly/2xZnuiF
  - **OREGON:** bit.ly/2czG1Vj
- See the instructions on page 60 for building your bonfire.
- Bring a thermos of warm drinks and snacks you can eat with your fingers.
- Bring camp chairs or stadium cushions and heavy blankets to help keep you warm.

Walnut Wish Boats

MAKES 12 WISH BOATS

Light and launch your walnut candle into the water with good wishes for the new year and thoughts of what you will do in the growing light of spring.

WHAT YOU WILL NEED:

Sharp knife

6 walnuts in the shell

2 white wax candles, each 8 to 10 inches long, or 1 sheet beeswax

Microwave-safe dish

Microwave, or hair dryer

Scissors

12 (1.5-inch) pieces cotton string

Matches

At home, split the walnuts into perfect halves by inserting the tip of the knife into the wider end of the nut and twisting slightly. Pick out the meat from the halves and save it to eat. Scrape out the shell with the knife. If you are using candles, cut them into 12 approximately 1-inch pieces. Place each piece into a walnut shell half, and set in a microwave-safe dish. When 4 or 5 of the shells are filled, place the dish in the microwave and zap for 30-second increments. The wax does not need to melt all the way; you can begin to press it into the shell when it is warm and pliable. Make sure there is enough wick for easy lighting.

If you can get your hands on a sheet of beeswax, it is even easier. Warm the wax using a hair dryer until it is pliable. Cut a 1-inch strip with scissors, press a piece of string in the middle, and roll the wax into a oval-shaped ball with the wick poking out. Press the warmed ball of wax and wick into the shell.

On the beach, find a calm launching place without big waves. Light your candle and place the boat into the water. Make a wish!

NEW YEAR'S DAY POLAR BEAR PLUNGE

Forget the resolutions, the promises you want to keep but never will. You may be a little bleary after New Year's Eve celebrations, but you won't regret jumping with your friends into the gray water in the morning.

The worst thing that could happen is to stay home nursing your hangover and feeling half dead. As you hurtle into cold water, there is a swift restriction of blood vessels, creating a robust cardiovascular pump throughout the body that surges blood from sole to crown, and suddenly you'll feel very much alive. Here are the best places for a public plunge:

British Columbia
- **NORTH VANCOUVER:** Deep Cove Panorama Park
- **VANCOUVER:** English Bay Bathhouse
- **WHITE ROCK:** White Rock Pier

Washington
- **KIRKLAND:** Marina Park
- **BAINBRIDGE ISLAND:** Lytle Beach
- **SEATTLE:** Matthews Beach Park
- **RENTON:** Gene Coulon Memorial Beach Park
- **TACOMA:** Point Defiance Marina boat launch

Oregon
- **MANZANITA:** Neahkahnie Beach
- **TILLAMOOK:** Oceanside Beach State Recreation Site

WHAT YOU WILL NEED:
Surf shoes, if you will
  be navigating a stony
  beach to the water
Big beach towel
Bathrobe or warm clothes
  that are easy to pull on
Thermos of something hot,
  for drinking afterward
Courage!

There is bravery in numbers, but if there is not a local polar plunge event near you, gather your friends and find the sea. Leave your dog at home, do not stay in the water longer than a few minutes, and have that thermos of hot drinks ready. All together now: jump!

THE SNOW GEESE OF FIR ISLAND

Picture hundreds of flying snow-goose skeins filling the sky on a rosy dawn and then settling into a field planted with grain just for them, as they cluck and bob and fill their bellies. Tens of thousands of snow geese migrate from the Arctic and overwinter on Fir Island in the Skagit Valley to gain fat and fuel for the 3,000-mile-long journey back to their nesting sites in the Arctic. Witnessing the flight blizzard of these snow-white birds against a winter dawn is a transcendent experience. The geese arrive on Fir Island in late November and stay until early spring. For more information, visit bit.ly/2rkcS92.

You need an early start for the best viewing, as the geese arrive at sunrise from their sleep on Skagit Bay. It is illegal to park on the side of the road to view them; instead, drive to the designated viewing area at the end of the road on the Fir Island Farms Reserve. You will need a Discover Pass to park here (see Resources, page 223).

CITIZEN SCIENCE: AUDUBON SOCIETY BIRD COUNTS

Christmas Bird Count

Every winter for the last 100 years, the Audubon Society has sponsored an early-winter census of birds. Thousands of volunteers across the United States and Canada take a 24-hour period between December 14 and January 5 to count the birds in a specific local area and supply vital information on bird populations and emerging trends.

There are guidelines for the count. You must register in advance with your local compiler and follow specified routes through a 15-mile-diameter circle. To sign up and for more information, visit bit.ly/2gJwcVV.

Great Backyard Bird Count

Want to stay in your backyard? The Audubon Society also sponsors the Great Backyard Bird Count on Presidents' Day weekend in February, when you can count the birds in your backyard and enter the results online. For more information, visit bit.ly/1AeW7ZL.

Park the car and walk the dike for a good view of both the bay and the fields of feeding geese.

Plan to spend several hours at the reserve, then treat yourself to lunch or a late breakfast in **La Conner** at Calico Cupboard Café and Bakery (CalicoCupboardCafe.com). La Conner itself is a worthy destination. This fishing town has morphed into an artists' colony over the years and today has twenty-one art galleries, three museums, and many waterfront restaurants and boutiques. Stop at the Chamber of Commerce to pick up a bird-viewing map.

Tips and Tricks

- Dress warmly, prepare for rain, and bring hats and gloves.
- Bring binoculars, a thermos of a warm beverage, water, snacks, camera, and a bird identification book.
- Watch for eagles, tundra swans, shorebirds, and water fowl.
- Do not try to rouse feeding geese into flight by walking toward them. Not only is it illegal, but the geese are adding fat reserves for their long migration back to the nesting grounds that must last through their fast while they incubate their eggs. Every flight diminishes their fat reserves.

STARGAZING BY THE SHORE

The first galaxies banged into existence over a billion years ago, and we are tucked inside one of them, the Milky Way galaxy. Here on planet Earth, Carl Sagan reminds us that everything—from our bodies to apples to the ground at our feet—is made of stardust, and that is reason enough to contemplate the vast night sky.

The shore in the Pacific Northwest is a fine place for sky watching, and clear winter skies make the fainter stars more visible. Choose a beach as far from city lights as possible, and the night sky will pop with galaxies and planets, especially with a pair of good binoculars or a small telescope. Download one of the many apps available for discovering and naming the constellations (Sky Guide is a good one). Point your phone at a star, and the app identifies it along with the constellation it is embedded in. There are many meteor showers during the winter months, but the three to watch for are the Leonids (November 17 to 18), the Geminids (December 13 to 14), and the Quadrantid (January 3 to 4).

MICRO-ADVENTURE: YURT CAMPING

Camping in a yurt on the Pacific Coast is comfort camping with heat! There are several state and county parks on the ocean in Washington and Oregon where you can rent yurts, as well as watch storms, beachcomb, surf, ride bikes, and more.

Washington
- SMOKEY POINT: Kayak Point County Park, bit.ly/2rtdcRm
- ABERDEEN: Grayland Beach State Park, bit.ly/2rk2EFK
- WESTPORT: Twin Harbors State Park, bit.ly/2rNXZxq
- LONG BEACH PENINSULA: Cape Disappointment State Park, bit.ly/2rqu516

Oregon
- HAMMOND: Fort Stevens State Park, bit.ly/1mDMpKU
- TILLAMOOK: Cape Lookout State Park, bit.ly/2qP46fC
- NEWPORT: Beverly Beach State Park, bit.ly/2rNGmxM

Here are a few of the major constellations and stars you may see:

ORION: The winter night sky is dominated by this constellation, easily picked out by looking in the southeast for three bright stars lined up in a row, forming Orion the Hunter's belt. Look closely and connect the star dots for his raised club and shield, his shoulders, and his legs. In his western heel burns the bright star Rigel. Look to the upper left of the belt, and you will find a bright-orange star called Betelgeuse (say "Beetlejuice").

CANIS MAJOR AND SIRIUS: Sirius is known as the Dog Star, the brightest star in the night sky. It makes up the head of Canis Major, the Great Dog constellation that accompanies Orion the Hunter. To find it, follow the line of Orion's belt to the left and you can't miss it.

CANIS MINOR AND PROCYON: Directly above Sirius is the star Procyon, part of the constellation Canis Minor, or Little Dog, with Orion. Follow the line of Orion's shoulder stars to the first bright star, which is Procyon.

BIG DIPPER AND POLARIS: Not actually a constellation but an asterism (a star pattern) that is part of the constellation Ursa Major (the Great Bear), the Big Dipper is one of the most familiar star shapes in the night sky. It also directs the eye to Polaris, the North Star, which has guided navigators for centuries, including African Americans escaping slavery by fleeing to northern states. Draw a straight line from the lip of the Big Dipper to find Polaris. It is at the end of the Little Dipper's handle.

PLEIADES: Also known as the Seven Sisters, this famous galactic star cluster is easy to find: follow Orion's belt to the right and up into this small but distinctive star cluster. Use binoculars for the best viewing.

CASSIOPEIA: A beautiful constellation mythologized as the queen who was too vain, this zigzag row of five bright stars in the northwest sky forms a giant W that looks like a La-Z-Boy recliner.

ORION

CANIS MAJOR

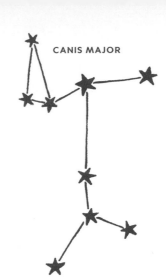

CANIS MINOR

Orion

Procyon

Betelgeuse

Winter
Triangle

Sirius

PLEIADES

Polaris

BIG DIPPER

CASSIOPEIA

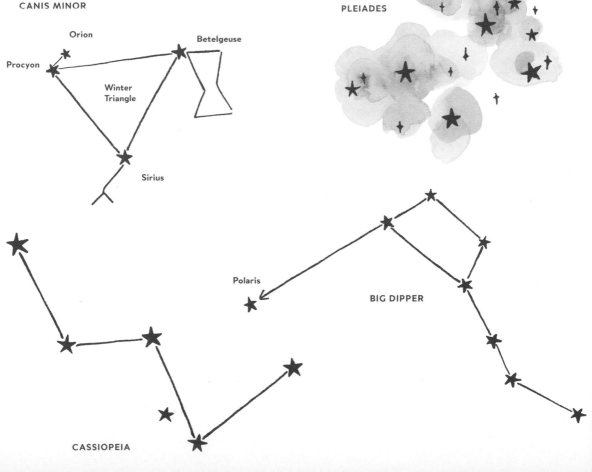

CITIZEN SCIENCE: MEASURE THE NIGHT-SKY BRIGHTNESS

Globe at Night is an international star-hunting program that addresses and raises awareness of light pollution by having citizens all over the world observe and report the night-sky brightness. Light pollution not only obscures discernible constellations and the meteor showers that make up our universe, but squanders a huge amount of energy. The beach is a good observation point, and the process is simple:

· Each month there is a 10-day campaign on clear and moonless nights to locate the constellation of the month. For example, in spring it is Leo, made up of the star "drops" that fall from the bottom of the Big Dipper.

· Download the Globe at Night app (bit.ly/1P2YPG0); find the constellation of the month and answer a few questions such as your location, cloud cover, and a comparison of the number of stars you see in the constellation with their series of charts showing progressively fainter stars. Submit the information and contribute to a growing body of data on the impact of light pollution.

· Dates for the 10-day campaigns each month change from year to year. For the current year, visit bit.ly/2s2lt06.

· Don't stand under or near a light.

· Allow your eyes to adjust to the dark for 20 to 30 minutes before entering observations. If light is necessary, use a flashlight covered with a red balloon (see Tips and Tricks).

· For more information on how to participate, visit GlobeatNight.org.

Tips and Tricks

- Bring blankets, camp chairs, hats and gloves, binoculars or small telescope, and a star chart or app like Sky Guide.
- Check the weather: clouds, smog, haze, and mist will impede your viewing. The app Clear Sky Chart forecasts the best nights for star gazing.
- Avoid viewing during a full moon, which washes out faint stars with its light.
- Make a red-light flashlight by stretching a red balloon over the lens of a flashlight that has an old-fashioned bulb (not an LED). Secure it into place with a rubber band. For best viewing, allow your eyes to adapt to the dark for 20 to 30 minutes, and if you need light, use the red-light flashlight. A red light will maintain the eyes' adaptation to darkness better than the white light from a regular flashlight.
- It takes about 30 minutes to begin to see stars after sunset. If you are at the beach as the sun lowers, you can time the light left until sunset using your hand. Hold your hand out at arm's length and bend your wrist with the palm horizontal and facing toward you. Line up the top length of your index finger with the bottom of the sun. Count the number of finger widths to the horizon. Each finger is approximately 15 minutes.

Festivals & Events

WINTERRUPTION

Shake off the rain and dull skies with this 3-day winter arts festival held in mid-February on Granville Island in Vancouver, British Columbia, featuring red-hot music, art exhibitions, fabulous food, and a maple sugar shack. There are free workshops and demonstrations that differ from year to year ranging from bookmaking to stone carving, and plenty of activities for kids. GranvilleIsland.com/Winterruption

FISHERPOETS GATHERING

Take the dazzling and dangerous world of commercial fishing, set it to story, poetry, or song in a wind-whipped seaside town, and you have the FisherPoets Gathering held the last weekend of February in **Astoria**, Oregon. This 3-day event is filled with the authentic voices of men and women connected to the fishing industry. From greenhorns to grizzled captains and slime liners to shipwrights, they all have a story to tell in the dim reaches of the Voodoo Room, the Wet Dog Café, or any one of the several other venues set aside for the weekend's events. The gathering also includes workshops on sea-chanty writing and knot tying, or go deep and take a class on ocean acidification. Tour a fishing boat; eat fresh seafood for breakfast, lunch, and dinner; wipe away a tear over the story of a son's death at sea; or belly laugh over a greenhorn's first day.

In our technologically driven world, the FisherPoet Gathering is a resounding tribute to the power of the spoken and sung word. It is a celebration of the fishing life and an ode to the Northwest. Don't miss it. FisherPoets.org

WALRUS AND CARPENTER
NIGHTTIME OYSTER PICNIC

Named after Lewis Carroll's poem "The Walrus and the Carpenter" ("O Oysters come and walk with us, a pleasant walk, a pleasant talk, upon the briny beach . . ."), this low-tide nighttime picnic hosted by Taylor Shellfish Farms as a benefit for the Puget Sound Restoration Fund is considered the ultimate oyster-eating experience. Several nighttime picnic events are held on minus tides (see page 8) in January and February, and they sell out fast. Depart on the Oyster Bus from Queen Anne in **Seattle** for the 90-minute ride to Totten Inlet in South Puget Sound for magic and moonlight while slurping local oysters freshly gathered at their peak. Olympia, Kumamoto, and Pacific oysters are shucked right there on the beach and paired with a deliciously crisp wine. As the tide rolls in, warm yourself at the bonfire with a cup of hot oyster stew before boarding the bus back to Seattle around midnight. The picnic is held no matter the weather because winter is the prime time for oyster lovers to feast: the oysters are firm and plump in the cold water. Even if you have to brave the elements for the picnic, it all benefits a great cause. bit.ly/1InQ3pH

STRANGE BREWFEST

Every January **Port Townsend**'s Strange Brewfest challenges Pacific Northwest brewers to come up with weird concoctions and then double dares the public to drink them. Squid ink, Dungeness crab, ghost chilis, and chicory are only a few of the creative ingredients added to brews. Dozens of established and emerging craft-beer and cider makers also offer up their more traditional best during the boisterous weekend. Expect terrific live music, chainsaw artists, fabulous seafood at local restaurants, and crowds. Do not expect the next Super Bowl sponsor. StrangeBrewfestPT.com

SMELT DERBY

Join **La Conner**'s Smelt Derby in February. Enjoy a smelt breakfast, run a 5K or 10K race, or print a fish (see page 100). There is a prize for the largest smelt caught! LaConnerRotary.org

SPRING

Outings

DAY BIKE TRIPS

Exploring the world at bike speed is liberating. You can stop when something catches your eye—a strange bird, a sunrise, a coffee shop—and it is inexpensive and good for the environment. Best of all you are outdoors, giving you a heightened sense of well-being. Now that the days are stretching longer and the smell of spring is in the air, it is time to head out for an all-day bike ride. Make it a weekend and mix it with a campout or a sweet place to stay, and watch the winter blues fade away.

Long Beach to Ilwaco on the Discovery Trail | *8.3 miles one way*

The best part of this outing, besides biking the gorgeous Discovery Trail, is staying at Sou'wester Lodge (SouwesterLodge.com) in **Seaview**, Washington. It is a place like no other—part funk, part bohemian, it has the goofy splendor of your granny's house shrunk down into a vintage trailer. Sou'wester Lodge is a historic lodge and a classic trailer resort that includes vintage trailers, small cabins, RV hookups and tent sites, and rooms in the main lodge, all minutes from the Pacific Ocean. There is an extensive vinyl record collection in the main lodge and a record player in most of the trailers for listening to them. Grab a classic like *Jimi Hendrix Greatest Hits*, the cribbage board, a few beers, and you have the makings of an exceptional evening.

The Sou'wester offers bikes you can borrow, though they may not be in the best condition, and you must bring your own helmet. Or you can rent bikes from Discovery Ride Shop (bit.ly/2qP9FLo) in **Long Beach** if you didn't bring your own.

From the Sou'wester Lodge, head a half mile west until you hit the ocean, where you'll pick up the Discovery Trail. Turn north to go to Long Beach if you want to start at the trail's official beginning, or turn south toward its end in **Ilwaco**. The Discovery Trail is considered one of the most beautiful bike rides in the Pacific Northwest. You will cycle on a paved path—and a stretch along a boardwalk—as you wind through grassy dunes along the shore and into the forest of Beards Hollow, before climbing then descending to Ilwaco.

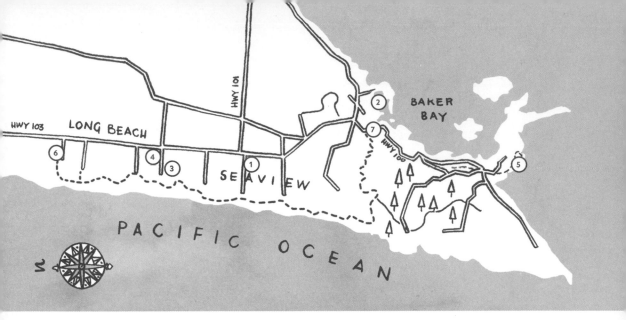

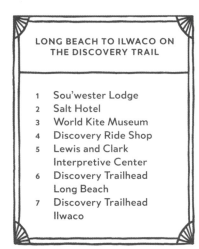

LONG BEACH TO ILWACO ON THE DISCOVERY TRAIL

1 Sou'wester Lodge
2 Salt Hotel
3 World Kite Museum
4 Discovery Ride Shop
5 Lewis and Clark
   Interpretive Center
6 Discovery Trailhead
   Long Beach
7 Discovery Trailhead
   Ilwaco

There are park benches, water, and bronze sculptures honoring Lewis and Clark's journey to the Pacific along the trail's 8.3-mile length. Take the side jaunt at Beards Hollow to the North Head Lighthouse in Cape Disappointment State Park if desired.

Extend your stay and:

- Take surf lessons from Skookum Surf Company (SkookumSurf.com), located in the Salt Hotel in Ilwaco.
- Wander through Cape Disappointment State Park: hike the many trails, visit the Lewis and Clark Interpretive Center, or go to North Head Lighthouse, the oldest operating lighthouse on the West Coast.
- Have dinner at the Depot Restaurant in Seaview, within walking distance of the Sou'wester Lodge. And in the end, head home filled up with the good life.

More Day Bike Trips: British Columbia

Seaside Greenway | *18 miles one way*
This exhilarating seaside path dedicated to walkers and cyclists includes the seawall at Stanley Park and runs along the shore through English Bay, False Creek, and Jericho Beach, to end at Spanish Banks. It is the world's longest uninterrupted waterfront path and begins at the Vancouver Convention Center downtown, at the north end of Burrard Street near the cruise-ship slips. The route is well marked. Start early and include a detour to Granville Island near False Creek and the Burrard Bridge. The Aquabus ferry (TheAquabus.com) accepts bicycles on the route across to Granville Island and the Granville Island Public Market, filled with a dizzying array of fruits, vegetables, artisan foods, local crafts, and fine wines and brews. Bring your panniers to fill up! Catch the ferry back, and pick up the Seaside Greenway to Stanley Park. Stop at a beach that catches your eye to feast on your Granville Island picnic, or pause at any of the dozens of cafés, coffee shops, and bistros you will pass on the way. There are many enticing detours along this route and you may want an extra day to complete it. For a map of the route, visit bit.ly/2syzv7m.

More Day Bike Trips: Washington

Guemes Island | *10-mile loop*
Guemes (pronounced "Gwem-ess") Island is technically a part of the **San Juan Islands** archipelago, but it lies in the shadow of the larger islands serviced by Washington State Ferries and is often overlooked. This sweet and sleepy island is a 5-minute ferry ride from **Anacortes** on an open ferry operated by Skagit County (bit.ly/2ugScNZ). Park near the ferry dock and cycle onto the boat. Once you arrive it is roughly 10 miles to circumnavigate the island. Start with a stop at the general store (bit.ly/2tj8fxR) near the ferry terminal for coffee and lunch supplies (it is closed Mondays and Tuesdays). It also has local beers on tap and baked goods. Head east on South Shore Road to Guemes Mountain trailhead, and park your bike for the 2.2-mile hike up the baby mountain of 500 feet elevation. In late spring there are sweeps of wild roses and other flowers along the rocky top. On your bike again, continue the loop north and check out the Guemes Island Resort (GuemesIslandResort.com) and its charming collection of cabins and yurts

at reasonable prices. It also has a small gift shop that sells snacks and ice cream. Continue around the island on West Shore Road, take a left on South Shore Road, and end up back at the ferry terminal. Sit on the porch at the general store and sip a cold beer before taking the boat back to Anacortes. For a map and more information, visit bit.ly/2snv0xo.

Whidbey Island | 14-mile loop
Whidbey Island is the perfect getaway for Seattleites, particularly if you are on a bicycle and can zip onto the ferry past the long lines of cars. The **Mukilteo** ferry is a 30-minute drive from **Seattle**, the boat ride is 20 minutes long, and then you will have a 14-mile bike day touring wineries. The first is in **Langley**, about 6 miles from the ferry dock, an irresistible little town with a great bookstore and tempting places to eat. Ott & Murphy (OttMurphyWines.com) is right on the water with a fabulous view of Saratoga Passage. Next stop, Bloom's Winery (BloomsWinery.com), about 4 miles along. After trying the cabernet, pedal about 2 miles to Whidbey Island Distillery (WhidbeyDistillery.com). Be sure to sample the loganberry liqueur! Last stop is Spoiled Dog Winery (SpoiledDogWinery.com), only a half mile from the distillery. The malbec is divine. The ride back to the **Clinton** ferry is a little over 4 miles.

Feel free to riff off this route. Explore more and camp out at Fort Ebey State Park, hike a section of the Pacific Northwest National Scenic Trail along the shore, or visit more wineries and make it a weekend. For maps and more information, visit bit.ly/2rkTWY1.

Sequim to Port Angeles on the Olympic Discovery Trail | 17 miles one way
The Olympic Discovery Trail (OlympicDiscoveryTrail.org) traverses nearly 130 miles across Washington's wild and scenic Olympic Peninsula, beginning in Port Townsend and ending at the Pacific Ocean. The section for your bike day trip begins in **Sequim** and continues 17 miles through fields and farms, over creeks and rivers, with a beautiful 4-mile stretch along the Strait of Juan de Fuca, to **Port Angeles**. Retrace the route for a 34-mile cycling day.

Begin at Railroad Bridge Park in Sequim and park the car. This scenic park is well known for bird-watching, and the Audubon center here has informative displays of local marine birds and wildlife. Stay hydrated! Fill up your water bottle here. On the way, there are several beach access

points along the Strait of Juan de Fuca where you can pause, stretch, and
enjoy the seascape before carrying on to Port Angeles and lunch at the
First Street Haven Restaurant (bit.ly/2tWtWB9). Bike along the city pier to
see if the fish are biting for the local fishers, then head back to Sequim. If
you are ready for dinner when you reach Sequim, do not pass up Nourish
(NourishSequim.com). It serves succulent garden-to-plate dishes that will
hit the spot after a day of biking. For maps and more information, visit
OlympicDiscoveryTrail.com.

Bainbridge Island | *14.2- or 19-mile loop*
Bringing a bike aboard a Washington State Ferries boat is a singular pleasure.
Head to the bow of the boat and park against the railings on either side. You
will be the first off the ferry. This daylong biking trip on **Bainbridge Island**
would not be complete without a good meal or two to fuel the trip. Begin
with breakfast at the Madison Diner (TheMadisonDiner.com) in **Winslow**
and enjoy the corn pancakes with slabs of bacon. Go north on Madison until
you hit State Route 305. Take a left (north), and at the first light take a right
onto North Madison Avenue. Stay right at the fork to Manitou Beach Drive
NE. This is a gorgeous stretch along the water with a stunning view of the
Seattle skyline. Take a left on Falk Road, and at its end take a left onto Valley
Road. You have arrived at historic **Rolling Bay**. Check out Bay Hay and Feed
(BayHayandFeed.com) for its eclectic offering of everything from chicken
feed to toys and outdoor gear. Via Rosa 11 Italian Kitchen (bit.ly/2tW7YOP)
is across the street, and even if you are not hungry, drop by to take home its
exceptional handmade pasta and tiramisu. Continue north on Sunrise Drive
for 3.7 miles, and turn right into Fay Bainbridge State Park to explore the

beach and fill up your water bottle. Continue north on Sunrise; the road will bend left (west) and turn into Lafayette Road. Go a half mile and take a left on Euclid Avenue. At the stop sign take a left (south) down Phelps Road for 2 miles until you hit SR 305. You can either bike the highway south back to the ferry, or cross it to Miller Road. After 3 miles on Miller Road, go left on High School Road and back to SR 305 to turn right (south) to the ferry. Here's a map of Bainbridge Island: bit.ly/2sPBIhJ.

Elliott Bay Trail | *22 miles round-trip*
This exceptional urban route via the Elliott Bay Trail will take you along the Seattle waterfront from Pier 90 through Myrtle Edwards Park to Alki Beach Park via the King County Water Taxi (bit.ly/2tjgXvs), for a 22-mile round-trip. You will pedal past many attractions—feel free to stop to explore Olympic Sculpture Park, the public fishing pier, the Ferris wheel, Ivar's (Ivars.com) for fish and chips, and Alki and its numerous shops and cafés. Begin by parking at Elliott Bay Marina and head downhill to Smith Cove Park. Pick up the trail beside the West Galer Street parking area (you can park here also). Once through Myrtle Edwards Park, cut across Alaskan Way to the east side, where there is a bike and pedestrian path. Follow the path to Pier 52, the ferry terminal, and the King County Water Taxi, and walk your bicycle aboard for **West Seattle**. The Alki Beach Park bike path, which you pick up right off the ferry, is classic Seattle. The entire trail is a paved path designated for bikes, hugging the water with breathtaking views of the Seattle skyline. Head west, take your time, then turn around at the far end of the path at Alki Beach Park and retrace your way back to Pier 90. For maps and more information, visit bit.ly/2syWvDp.

Dash Point State Park | *11 miles*
Dash Point State Park is a 398-acre park along Puget Sound with 11 miles of mountain biking trails through a mature forest. The trails are signed and graded for difficulty from easy to advanced. The trails are wide, single tracks that are popular with hikers; don't careen around blind corners! Access the trails at the day-use parking lot on Hoyt Road and don't forget to hang your Discover Pass (see Resources, page 223). The trails close at dusk. Find a trail map here: bit.ly/2lhW0Pc.

More Day Bike Trips: Oregon

Astoria Riverwalk | *6.4 miles one way*
The Astoria Riverwalk stretches along the city's waterfront for 6.4 miles. You can access the trail anywhere along its length. Along the way visit the fabulous Columbia River Maritime Museum. Head up the hill to Blue Scorcher Bakery and Café for lunch, then back down to the riverwalk. Cruise along listening to sea lions bark and sing under the trestles on the docks at 36th Street. The trail ends near the lagoons of Tongue Point. For maps and more information, visit bit.ly/2lhW0Pc.

MICRO-ADVENTURE: RENT A BOAT AND A CABIN ON AN ISLAND

Rent a cabin at Cama Beach State Park on **Camano Island**, Washington. They are charming, inexpensive, and right on the water. Rent a boat from the Center for Wooden Boats, located there, and motor out into Puget Sound to scoop a bucket of seawater to take home and make sea salt (see page 97), or hike the 15 miles of trails at nearby Camano Island State Park. Bird-watch, go crabbing, build a bonfire. bit.ly/2tYKQPJ

Catch it, Cook it, Eat it

SPOT PRAWNS

In the state of Washington, the recreational opportunity for harvesting spot prawns in Puget Sound is a brief blink of a day, maybe a few, in May. Oregon has no recreational spot-prawn harvest and British Columbia's spot prawns are a more sustainable and robust fishery, with the recreational harvest often open year round. But trapping them isn't easy. It takes local knowledge of the deep, rocky bottoms to know where to set the traps, and strength to haul up 400 feet of leaded line along with a trap weight the size of a small anchor. You will need a boat, perhaps a portable line puller, and a depth sounder. If you set out in Puget Sound, you may have to take a day off work for that single-day opening.

Save yourself time and money, and buy these exquisitely delicious shrimp when they first appear at the fish market in the spring. They are a true Northwest delicacy with firm and sweet flesh, reminiscent of a tender lobster. Spot prawns are not prawns; they are hermaphrodite shrimp that live for about 4 years. The first 2 years of life they are male, and the last 2 years they become female. You will recognize them at the market by the four white spots on their body—two on the head and two on the tail.

Tips and Tricks
- When a spot prawn dies, an enzyme in its brain releases, turning the flesh soft, so if possible buy spot prawns live. Look for lively prawns with strong tails; if the tail is curled, it indicates it is dying.
- Do not place live prawns in fresh water when you get home; it will kill them. Clean them as soon as possible after buying, or keep them in a cooler or on a bag of ice. Refrigerate for up to 4 hours.
- If you cannot find live spot prawns, buy them with their heads removed.
- Frozen spot prawns can be thawed in the refrigerator overnight.

Beer-Boiled Spot Prawns

MAKES 4 TO 5 SERVINGS

It is easy to overcook these treasures, so stand by the stove—they will take only a minute. Slightly underdone is perfect. Add a rhubarb pie for dessert, and you will be in Northwest springtime heaven.

INGREDIENTS:

4 (12-ounce) bottles lager

1 tablespoon sea salt

1 teaspoon whole black peppercorns

2 tablespoons fennel seeds

2 pounds whole spot prawns with heads removed, rinsed

Melted butter or cocktail sauce, for serving

In a large pot, add the lager, salt, peppercorns, and fennel, and stir to combine. Bring to a boil over high heat. Boil the mixture for 2 minutes to marry the flavors. Add the prawns, and cook for 40 seconds to 2 minutes, or until they turn pink and opaque. Using a slotted spoon, transfer the prawns to a bowl, and serve with the melted butter or a good cocktail sauce.

Grilled Fresh Spot Prawns with Sesame Oil

MAKES 4 TO 5 SERVINGS

This simple recipe makes a memorable feast if you are lucky enough to get your hands on live spot prawns. Frozen prawns work also; thaw them in the refrigerator before grilling. Invite your friends for this eat-with-your-hands food-fest, cover the table with newspaper, add a crusty loaf of bread, and serve with plenty of napkins.

INGREDIENTS:

2 pounds live spot prawns

2 tablespoons sesame oil

1 tablespoon coarse
  sea salt

1 teaspoon freshly
  ground black pepper

Seasoned rice vinegar
  (optional)

Preheat the grill to 400 degrees F. Place the live prawns on the grill, and cook for approximately 2 minutes on each side, or until the meat is white. To check for doneness, pull off a head and peek inside. Keep in mind that it is far better to undercook them than overcook—live spot prawns make coveted sashimi! Place the whole cooked prawns in a large bowl and toss with the oil, salt, and pepper. Add a splash of seasoned rice vinegar to taste.

PACIFIC NORTHWEST OYSTERS

The world is split into those who think oysters are nothing but sea goo and those who consider oysters seafood manna, especially slurped raw. If you belong to the latter category, you're in luck. The cold waters of the Pacific Northwest abound with oysters. Whether ordered in a local restaurant, bought at a farmers' market, or gathered on a public beach, these luscious bivalves are available in abundance.

Oyster Types and Terms

There are five species here in the Pacific Northwest:

- **PACIFIC:** These make up 90 percent of the oysters consumed here, but they are renamed depending on the location where they are grown, if they are tumbled, how they are harvested, what their salinity is, and other attributes contributing to their unique flavor. Naked Boy, Hama Hama, Little Skookum, and Fanny Bay are only a few among dozens of varieties of Pacifics you will encounter.
- **KUMAMOTO:** If you are trying a raw oyster for the first time, choose the Kuma. It is petite and plump, and the deep cup makes tipping it up and slurping it down easy. The flavor is subtle and the texture sublime.
- **VIRGINICA:** The first native eastern oyster grown in the Pacific Northwest, the Totten Inlet Virginica oyster is in a class of its own—quietly briny, juicy, flavorful, and rare because they are difficult to grow. If you see them on the menu, order them!
- **EUROPEAN FLAT:** Rowan Jacobsen, author of *A Geography of Oysters* (a book all oyster lovers should own) calls European Flats the Sean Penn of the oyster world—intense and memorable, but you wouldn't want to eat them every day. Don't make these your first raw oyster.
- **OLYMPIA:** This is the Pacific Northwest's only native oyster. It is tiny with flesh the size of a quarter; it has a distinctive, coppery, pennies-in-the-mouth taste that is exceptional.

These are good terms to know:

- "Tumbled" oysters are grown in bags that are tumbled around by tides, creating a deeper cup and a fatter oyster.
- "Merroir" is the coined word for oyster taste based on the French term "terroir," when wine erupts with the taste of the environment it was

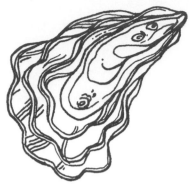

PACIFIC

KUMAMOTO

VIRGINICA

EUROPEAN FLAT

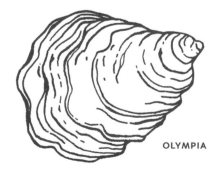

OLYMPIA

grown in. The location where oysters are grown will largely determine their flavor: minerals, salinity, algae, even the evergreens growing up a river can lend a subtle flavor to the merroir.

• "Liquor" is the natural juice within the oyster that helps to keep it alive when it is out of the water. This juice is an integral part of the taste sensation and should never be dumped from the shell before eating the oyster raw.

Oyster Tips

• Collect oysters on a minus tide at night at Dosewallips State Park (bit.ly/2qLvDUf) on Hood Canal. Build a bonfire, shuck them on the beach, then return to a warm cabin at the campground.
• Oysters should be closed tightly when you gather them on the beach or buy them.
• When picking oysters, look for the hinge, or "umbo," at the narrow end of the oyster. This is where you will enter and shuck the oyster, and some umbos are easier to find than others.
• If you are eating oysters raw, it's wise to heed the R rule: Don't eat them in months without an R in the name—May through August. Oysters spawn in warm months and their flesh tends to soften and get flabby. The warmer seawater can also develop higher bacteria counts ingested by the oysters. However, if you buy them to cook, or if they are triploids (basically a sterile hybrid), it really doesn't matter which month you eat them in.
• Store live oysters cup side down in the refrigerator, covered with a damp dish towel. Pacific and Kumamoto oysters will keep up to a week this way. Eat Olympias and European Flats as soon as possible.
• If you buy oysters, farmed is a better choice than wild. Oysters are filter feeders and are able to filter up to 50 gallons of seawater a day, cleaning up particulates and algae from oceans and waterways instead of polluting them like traditional fish farms. Oyster farms also help sustain wild native populations by satisfying market needs.
• For best eating, chill raw oysters for at least an hour on ice.
• Chew raw oysters and slurp down the liquor cupped in the shell with them.

Where to Go

These are some of the best beaches in British Columbia and Washington for oyster harvesting. Recreational oyster harvesting is not permitted in Oregon.

British Columbia
- **VANCOUVER ISLAND:** Baynes Sound, Kye Bay, Nanoose Bay

Washington
- **WHIDBEY ISLAND:** West Penn Cove
- **HOOD CANAL:** Dosewallips State Park, Duckabush State Park, Triton Cove Tidelands, Belfair State Park, Oyster Reserves of Oakland Bay
- **SOUTH PUGET SOUND:** Frye Cove County Park, North Bay

For a list of more oyster beaches in Washington State, visit bit.ly/2qTGd8w.

Equipment
- Shellfish license, for those 16 years and older (see Resources, page 223)
- Discover Pass for all Washington state parks (DiscoverPass.wa.gov)
- Gloves
- Shucking knife
- Bowl or small, clean bucket, set in a bucket of ice
- Dish towel

SHUCKING KNIVES

Techniques

To harvest oysters, you need a low tide (a minus tide—under 0 feet—is best; a 1-foot tide can work in some places. See How to Read a Tide Table, page 8). The greatest oysters you will ever eat are plucked off a tidal flat, shucked, and slurped right there standing in your rubber boots. Then throw the shells over your shoulder for luck and legal reasons. Anyone can do it; picking oysters on a low tide is like taking candy from a baby. But best to wait to harvest if it has been raining heavily; the runoff can contain contaminants ingested by the oysters. Always call the red tide hotline in your area to learn about beach closures before harvesting (see Paralytic Shellfish Poison, page 27).

Harvest the oysters close to the tide line or right in the water, where they will be cooler and fresher than oysters exposed to warm, ambient temperatures. Smaller oysters are good for eating raw, while the larger ones are best for cooking. The legal limit in the state of Washington is eighteen per day, fifteen in British Columbia, with a minimum size of 2.5 inches across the longest distance of the shell. Important: All Washington oysters gathered on the beach must be shucked there and the shells left in the place where you harvested them for future baby oyster spat to attach to. Place the shucked oyster meat in the bowl along with the liquor, and when you reach your limit, store the oysters in the refrigerator, in a covered container placed in a larger container filled with ice. Replenish the ice when it melts. The oysters will keep for up to a week.

How to Shuck an Oyster

Wrap the dish towel around the oyster, cup side down with the hinge (the narrow end) sticking out of the towel (see Figure 1). Use the oyster knife to burrow slowly and firmly into the hinge with a slight twisting motion, cup side down, until you feel the knife penetrate into the shell (see Figure 2). Twist the knife, and you will feel the shell give. Then slide the knife along the top shell to cut the adductor muscle that holds the meat in the shell (see Figure 3). Place the oyster and the precious liquor into the bowl.

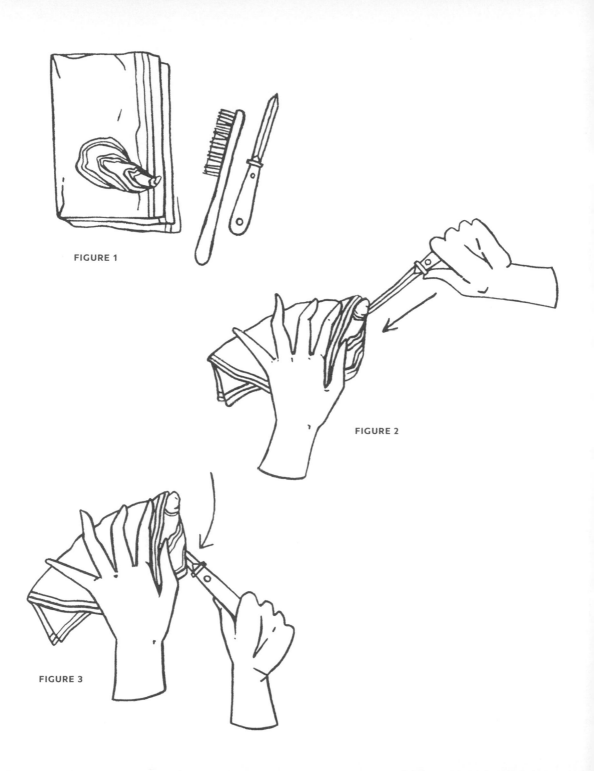

FIGURE 1

FIGURE 2

FIGURE 3

Simple Mignonette for Raw Oysters

MAKES ABOUT ¼ CUP, ABOUT ENOUGH FOR 1 DOZEN OYSTERS ON THE HALF SHELL

Raw oysters require few condiments. They are a unique food delivered to your mouth unadulterated, pure, and alive moments before eating, and it's best to keep it that way. At the most serve wedges of lemon or lime, a finely minced jalapeño pepper, and this simple mignonette.

INGREDIENTS:
2 tablespoons finely
 minced shallot
3 tablespoons
 champagne vinegar
Pinch granulated sugar

In a small bowl, mix the shallot, vinegar, and sugar together. Place a small amount on a raw oyster just before slurping.

Chargrilled Oysters

MAKES 3 SERVINGS

The oyster liquor and the butter mingle in this recipe into an unforgettable taste. For presentation, arrange the grilled oysters on a serving plate strewn with seaweed or on a pile of rock salt.

INGREDIENTS:
1 teaspoon lemon zest
½ teaspoon minced
 fresh mint
3 tablespoons melted
 unsalted butter
1 dozen shucked oysters
 on the half shell

In a small bowl, add the lemon zest, mint, and butter, and stir to combine. Fire up the grill, and preheat on high heat. Place the oysters on the grill. Using a pastry brush, liberally brush the melted butter on the meat, allowing some of the butter to drip onto the coals or hot grill to add a smoky taste. Close the grill lid, wait for 2 minutes, then check the oysters. When they are beginning to shrink and the butter is bubbly and browned around the edges, they are ready to eat.

Bacon-Wrapped Oysters (Angels on Horseback)

MAKES 4 APPETIZER SERVINGS

Even those ambivalent about oysters will enjoy these divine bacon-wrapped nuggets.

INGREDIENTS:

6 slices thick-cut bacon,
   cut in half
1 dozen shucked oysters
   removed from the shell

12 toothpicks
Sourdough Toast
   (recipe follows)

Preheat the oven to 500 degrees F. Wrap a slice of bacon around each piece of oyster meat, and secure with a toothpick. Place the wrapped oysters on a baking sheet, and bake for about 10 minutes, or until the bacon is browned. Serve each one on a square of sourdough toast.

Sourdough Toast

MAKES 12 TOASTS

INGREDIENTS:

½-inch-thick slices
   sourdough bread

½ cup salted butter, at
   room temperature

Preheat the oven to 375 degrees F. Cut the bread into 12 squares slightly larger than the wrapped oysters. Butter both sides of the squares and place on a baking sheet. Bake for about 10 minutes, or until the bottom is browned, then flip the squares and bake 5 minutes longer until the second side is browned.

Beach Projects

LAVENDER SEA SALT BODY SCRUB

MAKES JUST OVER 1 CUP

Sea salt body scrubs clean, exfoliate, and moisturize your skin at the same time. Use the sea salt made on page 97 for this simple recipe, or buy it from your grocer. You can adjust the number of drops of the essential oil for a stronger or more delicate scent.

WHAT YOU WILL NEED:
1 cup sea salt
½ cup coconut oil
10 to 15 drops lavender
   essential oil
Small jar with a lid
2 sprigs lavender

In a small bowl, add the sea salt, coconut oil, and essential oil drops, and stir together. Place the scrub in the jar. Settle the lavender sprigs into the salt and screw on the lid. Rub the scrub into your skin in the shower or bath, and rinse well. The scrub will keep indefinitely in a closed jar.

SEASHELL NIGHT-LIGHT

MAKES 1 NIGHT-LIGHT

So easy to make, this unique night-light casts a warm glow through a shell collected from the beach.

WHAT YOU WILL NEED:
Hot-glue gun
Small night-light with
  a plastic clip for
  mounting artwork
  (available on
  Amazon.com)

Medium-sized seashell
  approximately 3 inches
  across

Using the hot-glue gun, place glue on the straight piece of the plastic clip and along the bottom of the shell. Press the two together until cool. Plug in and enjoy!

DRIFTWOOD FORT

A hand-built driftwood fort is much more than wood stacked into a shelter: call it Zen, call it fun, call it a hands-on lesson in engineering. Kids won't be contemplating any of this while creating the fort—they will be too busy building!

There are many basic shapes to consider as you survey the potential in the driftwood stacks: A-frame, lean-to, dugout, teepee, log cabin, or simply wood leaned against a mother log. The process is self-directed and can be a satisfying collaboration between kids and adults.

Tips and Tricks
- Use only found materials from the beach and no tools.
- Start with bigger pieces of driftwood at the foundation and build from there.
- Bring a blanket and picnic supplies to the beach with you.
- Do not dismantle someone else's fort to make your own. You can remodel or add to it, however.

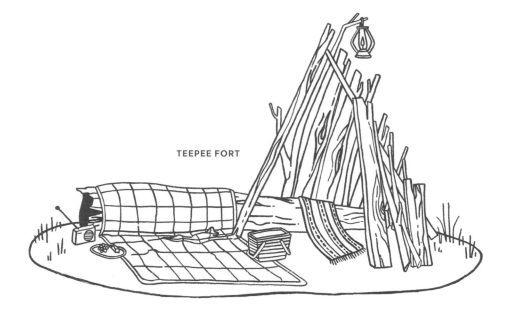

TEEPEE FORT

MESSAGE IN A BOTTLE

Writing a message in a bottle and throwing it into the sea asks for great patience in the face of expectation. The message may or may not be found; it will depend on many factors. But the project will inspire children's curiosity and help them learn more about the currents and tides of the Pacific Northwest. My son's message in a bottle was found forty miles away by a very nice woman who invited us to picnic on the beach where she found it. Include a dollar bill for the finder's effort to respond.

WHAT YOU WILL NEED:
Handwritten note
$1 bill
Clear glass wine bottle
    with a cork

On the note, have your child include the date, where you launched the bottle from, and a way to contact you. Ask to be informed where and when the bottle was found. Place the note and dollar in the bottle, cork it tightly, and launch it from shore, a bridge, a ferry, or a boat. Have patience! Your bottle may even float across the Pacific Ocean and take many months to reach a foreign shore.

On the Water

BOATING

There are moments on a perfect bluebird afternoon when something inside your land-dwelling self calls you to the water. There are abundant opportunities to answer that call and teach yourself to boat or sail, with or without your own boat. There are boat-share companies; places to rent a boat for an hour, an afternoon, or a weekend; and organizations and clubs offering navigation classes and on-the-water experience. Take advantage of the following boating resources, and find yourself somewhere else.

Boat Classes
Let's start at the beginning. You want to power that boat or sail that schooner like a pro, sweep along the water, and land at the dock smooth and sure. You want to be safe.

USPS Classes
The United States Power Squadrons (BeyondBoating.org) offers classes that make it possible. USPS is the largest nonprofit boating organization in the United States, with a mission to bring boating safety and knowledge to all interested people through classes and on-the-water instruction. Don't be intimidated by the name; it is for novices as well as those with experience. Northwest Boater Training (NWBoaterTraining.com) is the local affiliate of USPS in the Northwest, and it offers courses at very reasonable prices.

The classes include:
- Powerboat Handling
- Seamanship (for both powerboats and sailing)
- Piloting
- Navigation
- Weather
- Cruising and Cruise Planning
- Engine Maintenance
- Marine Electrical Systems
- Sailboats and Sailing Theory

Canadian Power and Sail Squadrons Classes
Northwest Boater Training's affiliate in British Columbia is Canadian Power and Sail Squadrons (bit.ly/2rlckQl). Note that Canada requires an operator of any power vessel to carry a Pleasure Craft Operator Card (PCOC).

Their courses include:
- Boating Basics (take this to receive your required PCOC)
- Introduction to Marine Navigation
- Boating Essentials
- Maritime Radio
- Radar classes
- Boat and Engine Maintenance
- Sailing

Boat Sharing and Rentals
Boat sharing is growing in popularity. It makes sense: I have a boat I don't use, and you want to use a boat but don't own one. There are dozens of boats available online up and down the Salish Sea, including yachts, kayaks, and sailboats. Just type in the location you would like to rent from, and a list of available boats will appear. Here are a couple companies to get you started:

Online companies
- **GETMYBOAT:** GetMyBoat.com
- **BOATSETTER:** Boatsetter.com

NAUTICAL TERMS

- **ABEAM**: Right angles to the ship's keel, but not actually on the boat
- **ABOVE BOARD**: Above the deck and in plain view
- **AFT**: Toward the back of the boat (astern)
- **AID TO NAVIGATION (ATON)**: Any marker that helps in navigation, including lighthouses, fog signals, and beacons
- **BEAM**: The greatest width of the boat
- **BEARING**: The direction of an object shown on a chart relative to the heading of a boat
- **BILGE**: The interior space of the hull of a boat below the floorboards
- **BITTER END**: The very last part of a rope or chain
- **BOOM**: The horizontal pole that extends from the bottom of the mast of a sailboat to secure the bottom of a sail
- **BOW**: The front of the boat
- **BOWLINE KNOT**: A knot used to make a temporary loop at the end of a line (rope)
- **BRIDGE**: The place on a boat from which it is steered and speed controlled
- **DRAFT**: The distance from the surface of the water to the lowest point of your boat
- **FATHOM**: 6 feet
- **FENDER**: A cushion-type object placed between the boat and a pier to prevent damage
- **GIVE-WAY VESSEL**: The boat that must yield to another boat
- **JIBING**: Turning the sailboat's stern so the wind changes from one side to the other (the opposite of tacking)
- **KNOT**: A measure of speed equal to 1 nautical mile (6,076 feet) per hour
- **LATITUDE**: The distance in degrees north or south of the equator
- **LEE (ALEE)**: The side sheltered from the wind
- **LONGITUDE**: The distance in degrees east or west of the meridian at Greenwich, England
- **NAUTICAL MILE**: One minute of latitude
- **PORT**: The left side of a boat as you face the bow
- **RUDDER**: Located under or behind the boat, a flat piece of wood, fiberglass, or metal used to steer the boat
- **SECURE**: To make fast or tie up
- **SPRING LINE**: A line that runs from a boat (usually abeam) when tied up to a pier or dock to prevent a backward and forward movement
- **STAND-ON VESSEL**: The boat that has the right-of-way
- **STARBOARD**: The right side of a boat as you face the bow
- **STERN**: The back of the boat
- **STOW**: To put an item in its place
- **TACKING**: Turning the sailboat's bow so the wind changes from one side of the boat to the other (the opposite of jibing)
- **TRIM**: Balancing the bow and stern of a boat to make moving through water more efficient depending on the kind of boat hull
- **WAKE**: The waves a boat leaves behind as it moves through water

British Columbia

VANCOUVER

- **GRANVILLE ISLAND BOAT RENTAL** (BoatRentalsVancouver.com): Powerboat rentals and crab supplies to drop a pot on your adventure.

VICTORIA

- **PEDDER BAY MARINA** (bit.ly/2rlbwuO): Powerboat rentals for fishing and sightseeing.

SIDNEY AND VANCOUVER

- **COOPER BOATING** (CooperBoating.com): Cooper Boating offers a wide range of classes for people from beginning sailors and powerboat wannabes to hard-core, experienced boaters looking to hone their skills. Fleets of sailboats and powerboats available to rent.

Washington

BELLINGHAM

- **COMMUNITY BOATING CENTER** (BoatingCenter.org): This splendid, volunteer-driven boating center has no memberships and no dues. The classes are open to the community and focus on small-boat recreation on Bellingham Bay. The center offers kayaks, paddleboards, rowboats, sailing dinghies, and keelboats for rent at very reasonable prices.
- **SAN JUAN SAILING** (SanJuanSailing.com): Classes and rentals of both sailboats and powerboats. It is easy access to the San Juan Islands from here.

SEATTLE

- **SEATTLE BOAT SHARE** (bit.ly/2ru7ezx): A local Seattle company that runs like a club. You can join at no cost to take various powerboat lessons for a fee, or step it up to the Full Sharepass membership to have access to unlimited weekday bookings as well as two weekend or holiday bookings at one time. It also offers a Group Sharepass and a weekday-only pass that is less expensive.
- **CENTER FOR WOODEN BOATS** (bit.ly/2s3kopX): Rent large or small sailboats inexpensively by the hour after a sailboat checkout with one of the staff (scheduled online).

- **WINDWORKS SAILING AND POWERBOATING** (WindworksSailing.com): This sailing club is located in Shilshole Bay Marina in Ballard as well as in Anacortes during the summer months for easy cruising to the San Juan Islands. It is far pricier than the United States Power Squadron classes but the services are extensive: sailing and powerboat lessons include on-the-water experience with the club's boats, and a fleet of both sailboats and powerboats are available to rent and use your new skills on, with pay-as-you-go fees once you join the club.

TACOMA

- **POINT DEFIANCE MARINA** (bit.ly/2rutwS5): Operated by Metro Parks Tacoma, this one-stop marina has it all: low-fee rental skiffs with 9.9-horsepower engines, kayaks, paddleboards, and a wide range of classes and events—such as fishing basics, crabbing, squid jigging, and saltwater fly-fishing—to enhance your experience on the water.

OLYMPIA, GIG HARBOR, SEATTLE

- **ISLAND SAILING** (IslandSailing.org): Island Sailing is a club founded by a group of passionate sailors that has expanded to offer a wide variety of classes, a fleet of sailboats to rent, and on-the-water training at reasonable prices. Its comprehensive sailing program will set you up with solid experience and a boat to use. Nonmembers can rent 20- to 22-foot boats for day sailing.

Oregon

LINCOLN CITY

- **BLUE HERON LANDING** (BlueHeronLanding.net): Offers runabouts, motorboats, pontoon boats, kayaks, and canoes for rent by the hour or the day.

SEATTLE CENTER FOR WOODEN BOATS

Seattle's Center for Wooden Boats (CWB) in South Lake Union is a Northwest treasure. CWB was founded in the late 1970s by Dick and Colleen Wagner when they turned their growing collection of traditional wooden boats into a hands-on maritime museum where the boat exhibits were not set behind glass or in a building, but were placed in the water where people could actually use them. It is free (donations encouraged) to look over the boats, participate in the boat-skills workshops, and join the Sunday Public Sail, where you can sail or motor in iconic boats, including a Bristol Bay gillnetter, on Sundays. The boat rides run rain or shine throughout the day and last about 45 minutes to an hour. There are no reservations, and on sunny days and holidays there can be long wait times. If you are impatient, rent your own boat for a small fee and head out.

The Center for Wooden Boats also offers fantastic opportunities to explore life on the water; learn to repair, navigate, and sail or run a boat; and attend skills workshops. In addition, sailing classes for all skill levels and ages are offered here, as well as in Medina Beach Park, Newcastle Beach Park, and Cama Beach State Park. The Center for Wooden Boats at Cama Beach State Park also rents out crab traps during crab season. Volunteers at CWB can earn 1 hour of free boat use for every 3 hours volunteered. Take advantage of this extraordinary foundation and learn what makes the Northwest a singular place to spend time. CWB.org

Celebrations & Nature

APRIL'S SHOOTING STARS: LYRID METEOR SHOWER

The Lyrid meteor shower is the year's first good meteor sky show that lasts from about April 16 to 25, peaking close to April 22 depending upon the year. Admittedly, the Pacific Northwest's moody spring cloud cover can hamper the view, but given the range of days, the odds are good there will be a break in the predawn sky to catch these ephemeral blasts of light. The Lyrid meteors are about as bright as the stars in the Big Dipper; you can expect around ten to fifteen meteors per hour, but the Lyrids are notoriously unpredictable and can offer fewer or a surge of up to one hundred per hour. Those rare outbursts are hard to forecast, but are one of the reasons to tip your head back to the night sky in April. Look toward the northeast. You do not need any special equipment; your eyes offer the largest field of view.

SPRING FIREBALLS

The spring equinox is fireball season. Fireballs are extraordinarily bright meteors that appear larger and longer than typical meteors and are often reported as UFOs for their neon colors and long, bright descent. NASA is not sure why there are more around the spring equinox than any other time of the year, but you may see them while watching the night sky for the Lyrids. Consider it a beautiful mystery if you catch sight of one.

EXPLORE THE TIDE POOLS OF SPRING

There is a window of time in spring and summer when the sea pulls back on a minus tide (see page 8) to reveal an intertidal zone filled with dazzling marine plants and animals. The tide pools of the Salish Sea and the Oregon coast are some of the most diverse and rich intertidal habitats on earth, and they are yours to explore on a low tide. You don't need special equipment or knowledge; however, a good illustrated guide, like *Fylling's Illustrated Guide to Pacific Tide Pools* by Marni Fylling, will enrich your experience and enable you to identify all the sea flora and fauna you encounter. Is that a blob of goo or a brooding anemone? Another bonus of a spring minus tide is the sudden access to rocks and caves that are covered by water during the day for most of the year: more to explore, more to discover, a secret world at your wet feet.

Tips and Tricks

- Tides vary up and down the coast. Look up a site-specific tide table (see How to Read a Tide Table, page 8) to earmark a tide that is 0 feet or lower for the beach you want to visit.
- Bring a magnifying glass to examine the marine life closely.
- Bring a bag with you to pick up any trash or litter you find, and haul it out.
- Wear shoes with good traction; the rocks can be slippery.
- Although many tide pools are exposed on a normal low tide, target the lowest tides for the most diversity of marine life.
- Watch your step! Walk only on sand whenever possible to avoid damaging these fragile ecosystems.
- Touch the marine life gently, preferably with one wet finger.
- Replace any rock you lift exactly the way it was.
- Do not bring shells or animals home.

Best Beaches for Tide Pools

Most beaches reveal interesting marine life at low tide. You can make it easy, go local, and check out a shore near you, or pack a picnic, jump in the car, and drive to one of the beaches listed below for an up-close and personal encounter with the briny treasures of the Pacific Northwest. Keep in mind all Washington state parks require a Discover Pass. In Oregon, buy a state park day-use parking permit (see Resources, page 223).

British Columbia
- VANCOUVER: Lighthouse Park, Spanish Banks, Third Beach, Kitsilano Beach
- TOFINO: Chesterman Beach, MacKenzie Beach, Lismer Beach
- WHITE ROCK: White Rock Beach
- PORT RENFREW: Botanical Beach
- VICTORIA: Cattle Point Urban Star Park

Washington
- BELLINGHAM: Larrabee State Park
- ORCAS ISLAND: Obstruction Pass State Park
- SAN JUAN ISLAND: Grandmas Cove, Cattle Point Natural Resources Conservation Area, Lime Kiln Point State Park
- WHIDBEY ISLAND: Double Bluff State Park, Deception Pass State Park
- PORT ANGELES: Salt Creek Recreation Area
- OLYMPIC PENINSULA: Rialto Beach (Hole-in-the-Wall), Shi Shi Beach, La Push beaches, Ruby Beach, Kalaloch Beach
- SHORELINE: Richmond Beach Saltwater Park
- SEATTLE: Golden Gardens Park, Discovery Park (north end of the beach), Constellation Park, Lincoln Park
- BURIEN: Seahurst Park
- VASHON ISLAND: Point Robinson Park
- DES MOINES: Saltwater State Park
- TACOMA: Titlow Park, Owen Beach at Point Defiance Park

Oregon:

- **CANNON BEACH:** Haystack Rock, Arcadia Beach State Recreation Site
- **MANZANITA:** Short Sands Beach at Oswald West State Park
- **PACIFIC CITY:** Cape Kiwanda State Natural Area
- **NEWPORT:** Yaquina Head Outstanding Natural Area (Quarry Cove, Cobble Beach)
- **SEAL ROCK:** Seal Rock State Recreation Site
- **YACHATS:** 804 Trail, Basalt Gateway, Spouting Horn, and the town beaches (there are tide pools everywhere in Yachats!)

MICRO-ADVENTURE: ATTEND TIDE-POOL CLINICS

Lincoln City, Oregon, offers guided tide-pool clinics throughout the spring. The 2-hour clinics are held on the beach and include valuable information and identification of marine wildlife while you explore the local pools. On your own, drive to Roads End State Recreation Site (bit .ly/2tluAdV), 4 miles north of town, and walk the beach north to the headland. The extraordinary tide pools are around the headland and accessible at low tide, but be sure to watch for the incoming tide and return before it covers your route back. From mid-October to Memorial Day, Lincoln City sponsors Finders Keepers where handcrafted glass floats are randomly placed on 7.5 miles of beach from Roads End to Siletz Bay for beachcombers to find. The number of floats placed is reflected by the year—2,018 for example. Keep your eyes out, you could get lucky!

Festivals & Events

CELEBRATE SEAFOOD!

There is a plethora of spring festivals honoring the briny seafood bounty of the Pacific Northwest. Crack a crab, chow down on razor-clam chowder, buy spot prawns fresh off the boat, and learn how to shuck an oyster or clean a clam.

British Columbia

Vancouver | Spot Prawn Festival and Boil
This one-of-a-kind festival celebrates the luscious spot prawn in mid-May. It is held at the False Creek Fishermen's Wharf near Granville Island, which has famed markets. The boil the festival is named after is a feast of spot prawns and delicious side dishes. There are spot-prawn cooking classes taught by local chefs and the opportunity to buy the prawns fresh off boats at the dock. The festival is free, but buy tickets for the boil in advance; they sell out fast! SpotPrawnFestival.com

Washington

Whidbey Island | Penn Cove MusselsFest
The Penn Cove MusselsFest in **Coupeville** honors the celebrated Penn Cove mussels, known for their sweet flavor and perfect texture. Held the first weekend in March, this festival includes tours to the rafts where mussels are grown, cooking demonstrations, a mussel-eating contest, and live music all weekend long. ThePennCoveMusselsFestival.com

Lilliwaup | Hama Hama Oyster Rama
Located on **Hood Canal**, the Hama Hama Oyster Rama is legend. If you love oysters, this is the festival for you. It is one big subtidal party where you can pick oysters and clams from the beach, watch a shucking contest, listen to

live music, and sip a brew in the beer garden. Attendance is limited and the festival is popular. The Oyster Rama is a one-day event usually held late April or early May. Start checking the website in March to buy tickets. While you are at it, buy tokens to purchase food, drinks, and the famous Blue Pool oysters, or plan on bringing cash. bit.ly/1IGbSvV

Long Beach | *Long Beach Razor Clam Festival*
The Long Beach Razor Clam Festival, held mid-April, offers everything razor clam: how to dig and clean them, and lush ways to cook them. Where else will you find a clam fritter cook-off and chef chowder wars? The festival offers a beer garden, live music, and kids' activities. Make a weekend of it and book reservations early at Sou'wester Lodge, a few miles south in **Seaview**; ride your bike down the Discovery Trail (see Long Beach to Ilwaco on the Discovery Trail, page 175) to the festival. Don't miss it! LongBeachRazorClamFestival.com

Oregon

Astoria | *Astoria Warrenton Crab, Seafood & Wine Festival*
This one is big and a bit more corporate than the quirky local fests. The crowds can top sixteen thousand but the festival includes a 30-year-old legendary crab feed. It is held the last weekend in April at the Clatsop County Fair & Expo Center and offers a sweep of Northwest wines, artisan cheeses, art, and seafood microcannery delicacies you will not find in many places. AstoriaCrabFest.com

SPRING WHALE WATCH WEEK IN OREGON

Each spring tens of thousands of gray whales migrate north from their breeding grounds in the Baja Peninsula, Mexico, to Alaska. The northward-migrating whales stay close to shore, usually within a half mile, and move at a slower pace than when they head south to Baja, offering splendid shows of breaching and spy-hopping along the way. Oregon celebrates the annual migration with Whale Watch Week every mid-March, with over two dozen designated sites along the coast where volunteers trained by the organization Whale Watching Spoken Here (WhaleSpoken.org) share the scoop on grays. The volunteers' hours are from 10:00 a.m. to 1:00 p.m. at many of the sites listed below as well as other places up and down the coast. For a complete list of whale-watching sites, visit bit.ly/2qS12zs.

Your first stop should be **Depoe Bay** and the Whale Watching Center, the hub for learning about gray whales. Plan on staying at the Inn at Spanish Head, near Lincoln City, for fabulous whale watching from your room or the lobby on the tenth floor. Head out to one of the following locations for the best chance of catching sight of these majestic leviathans.

- Cape Disappointment State Park
- Ecola State Park
- Cape Lookout State Park
- Spanish Head
- Cape Perpetua Interpretive Center
- Cooks Chasm turnout
- Sea Lion Caves turnout
- Umpqua Lighthouse
- Shore Acres State Park
- Face Rock State Scenic Viewpoint
- Cape Ferrelo

PACIFIC RIM WHALE FESTIVAL

This mid-March multiweek celebration of whales in **Ucluelet** and **Tofino**, British Columbia, includes science, art, parades, and Zodiac tours to a local hot spring with a naturalist—all celebrating the migration of whales to their Alaska summer feeding grounds. Join a curator collecting specimens for an aquarium and a First Nations guided canoe paddle to a traditional whaling village site; participate in the Blessing of the Boats and beach tug-of-war. And, of course, watch for whales. Make accommodation reservations early; this is a popular event. PacificRimWhaleFestival.com

KITE FESTIVALS

Kites are useless, beautiful things that hang in the sky by a thread; and that is why we love them—for their reckless beauty that serves no purpose other than play. The following festivals roll out the red carpet for the love of kites and allow us to marvel at the creativity and imagination of those who understand the importance of things that fly.

NOTE: Start flying your kite in spring, but the following festivals are held in summer. Mark your calendars!

British Columbia

Vancouver | Pacific Rim Kite Festival
You just might get lucky and see Vancouver's Ray Bethell flying three stunt kites at once—one attached to his waist and one in each hand, a world record (managing one stunt kite is incredibly difficult). He has even been known to fly thirty-nine kites at once. For 2 days in early June at Vanier Park, the Pacific Rim Kite Festival offers kite wars, kite flying set to music, and a kids' kite-making workshop, as well as demonstrations of some incredible feats of kite arabesque. The British Columbia Kitefliers Association sponsors the festival and has plenty of members on hand to get you started with eyes to the sky. bit.ly/2qSbyGX

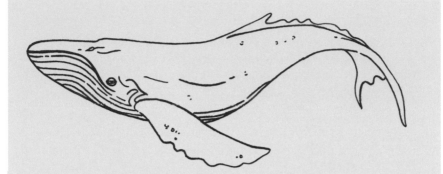

GRAY WHALE FACTS

- Grays are baleen whales, which means they have no teeth, just baleen plates. They scoop for small crustaceans along the ocean floor, gathering sediment and water that they force out through those beautiful baleen plates hanging from the sides of their jaws.
- The spout you see is not a discharge of water, but warm, moist air forcefully exhaled from their lungs that condenses as it meets the ambient air.
- All baleen whales have two spout holes, while whales with teeth have one.
- Gray whales have a rhythmic breathing pattern during migration: several short, shallow dives of 15 to 30 seconds, followed by a deep dive of 3 to 6 minutes. If you see the flukes, or tail fins, it usually means the whale is about to dive deep.
- Whales cannot fully fall asleep because they need to surface to breathe; instead, half of their brain sleeps while the other half remains conscious to signal the need for air when necessary.

Parksville | Parksville Lions International Kite Festival
This 2-day festival is held mid-July and includes a kite-building tent for beginners, kite-flying demonstrations, food concessions, and a "teddy bear drop" for kids: teddy bears with little parachutes are strung up on the strings of a large kite, then released, dropping to the outstretched hands of some lucky children. ParksvilleBeachFest.ca

Washington

Long Beach | Washington State International Kite Festival
The granddaddy of all kite festivals in the Pacific Northwest, the Washington State International Kite Festival is not to be missed. **Long Beach** is the hub of kite flying and home to the World Kite Museum, which has curated a fascinating exhibition of kites from all over the world and their use through history. The museum-sponsored festival runs for a week in mid-August and offers a dazzling display of kite trains, fierce sky battles, kite ballet set to music, and stunt kites that perform aerial tricks that will take your breath away. There are activities for kids including a lollipop drop and a kite-making camp. And don't miss the lighted kite night fly with fireworks afterward! KiteFestival.com

Oregon

Lincoln City | Lincoln City Summer Kite Festival
More kite demonstrations, kids' kite making, and performances by featured fliers. The festival is held the last weekend of June. bit.ly/1zt7uuu

Acknowledgments

This book began as an idea of my keen editor, Hannah Elnan, and I am filled with gratitude that she passed it on to me. Adventure is doubled when you have good company, and I hit the jackpot with my family and friends as we explored and researched the Pacific Northwest. Their wide-open enthusiasm for detours was inspiring. Big thank-you to Jenna, Nick, Ben, Molly, Daniel, Bridgette, Casi, and Nick, and to my frisky grandchildren for showing me how to explore like a kid.

There are those who added depth to the book with their time and hospitality: Marti, my drop-everything-and-go comrade; Suzie and Bill, who gave me the insider's guide and a place to stay on Lopez Island; Anne, who offered a room with a view while I adventured on Vancouver Island; Daniel, who shared his salmon-fishing expertise; and the countless strangers I met who have no idea how their passion and kindness bowled me over. The Pacific Northwest is not only beautiful but filled with good people.

Thank you to the brilliant chef Susan Banks for helping me develop the salmon recipes, and endless appreciation to Nick Hall, my son-in-law and gifted photographer, who generously offered the time from his busy schedule to capture the cinematic splendor of the Pacific Northwest.

Resources

Fishing Licenses
BRITISH COLUMBIA: bit.ly/2qe26OG
WASHINGTON: FishHunt.DFW.Wa.gov
OREGON: DFW.State.Or.us
/online_license_sales

Parking Permits for Recreational Sites
BRITISH COLUMBIA: bit.ly/2gr0C1z
WASHINGTON: DiscoverPass.wa.gov
OREGON: bit.ly/1QGYgaJ

Shellfish Biotoxin Assistance
BRITISH COLUMBIA: bit.ly/U5b8ML or
call 1-866-431-3474
WASHINGTON: bit.ly/1QmdXoF or call
1-800-562-5632
OREGON: bit.ly/1EhDcU6 or call
1-800-448-2474

Fish Openings and Regulations
BRITISH COLUMBIA: bit.ly/2qRZvtu
WASHINGTON: bit.ly/2tzfwub
OREGON: bit.ly/2utdyaR

Ferry Information
BRITISH COLUMBIA: BCFerries.com
WASHINGTON: WSDOT.Wa.gov/ferries, ClipperVacations.com

Boating Education
BRITISH COLUMBIA: bit.ly/2rlckQl
WASHINGTON: USPS.org
OREGON: bit.ly/2viDJkt

Weather Service
BRITISH COLUMBIA: Weather.gc.ca
WASHINGTON AND OREGON:
Weather.gov

Astronomical Societies
BRITISH COLUMBIA: Victoria.RASC.ca
WASHINGTON: SeattleAstro.org
OREGON: RoseCityAstronomers.net

Tides
ONLINE TIDE TABLE: Tide-Forecast.com

Burn Bans
BRITISH COLUMBIA: bit.ly/2s0iXp5
WASHINGTON: bit.ly/2xZnuiF
OREGON: Call 1-800-551-6949

appendix

SPECIES HARVEST CALENDAR
FOR THE PUGET SOUND REGION

	JANUARY	FEBRUARY	MARCH	APRIL	MAY
CLAMS‡	★★	★★	★★	★★★	★★★
RAZOR CLAMS‡‡	★★★	★★★	★★	★★	★★
SQUID‡‡‡	★★	★	✕	✕	✕
KING SALMON	✕	✕	★	★	✕
BLACKMOUTH SALMON	★★★	★★★	★★	★★	✕
SILVER SALMON	✕	✕	✕	✕	✕
SOCKEYE SALMON	✕	✕	✕	✕	✕
PINK SALMON	✕	✕	✕	✕	✕
CHUM SALMON	✕	✕	✕	✕	✕
CRAB‡‡‡‡	✕	✕	✕	✕	✕
SPOT PRAWNS	✕	✕	✕	✕	★★★
OYSTERS‡	★★★	★★★	★★★	★★★	★

×	CLOSED OR NOT IN SEASON	
★	FAIR	
★ ★	GOOD	
★ ★ ★	BEST	

JUNE	JULY	AUGUST	SEPTEMBER	OCTOBER	NOVEMBER	DECEMBER
★ ★ ★	★ ★ ★	★ ★ ★	★ ★ ★	★ ★ ★	★ ★ ★	★ ★ ★
×	×	×	×	★ ★	★ ★	★ ★ ★
★	★ ★	★ ★	★ ★	★ ★	★ ★ ★	★ ★ ★
★ ★	★ ★ ★	★ ★ ★	★	×	×	×
★	★	★	★ ★	★ ★	★ ★ ★	★ ★ ★
★	★ ★ ★	★ ★ ★	★ ★ ★	★ ★	★	×
★	★	★	×	×	×	×
×	★ ★ ★	★ ★ ★	★ ★	×	×	×
×	×	★	★	★ ★	★ ★	★ ★
★	★	★ ★	×	★ ★	★ ★	★ ★
×	×	×	×	×	×	×
★	★	★	★ ★ ★	★ ★ ★	★ ★ ★	★ ★ ★

‡Clam and oyster harvesting is open year round (except for razor clams) and subject to red tide closures; however, the low tides best for harvesting during the daylight hours are in the spring and summer. The best-tasting oysters are harvested in cooler months.

‡‡The setting of recreational razor-clam openings is complicated due to a variety of factors, from increasing marine toxins to sustainability. Each year varies from complete closure for the year to up to thirty-five openings. Always check for openings. **British Columbia:** bit.ly/2qRZvtu; **Washington:** bit.ly/1ev7K2F; **Oregon:** bit.ly/2qLdYrH.

‡‡‡Squid begin to arrive from the Strait of Juan de Fuca in late June, with Port Angeles usually hit first. They then move south into Puget Sound throughout the fall and the winter.

‡‡‡‡In Washington State, the recreational crab season changes every year, but generally it is divided into the summer crab season and the winter crab season. In Oregon, it is generally open year round. Crab molt in early summer and have less meat. Be aware there are years when the season is very limited. Always check for openings. **British Columbia:** bit.ly/2qRZvtu; **Washington:** bit.ly/1wVIpsj; **Oregon:** bit.ly/2qLdYrH.

Index

Note: Page numbers in *italic* refer to illustrations.

A

Anacortes, 7, 177–178
Arcadia Point, 13
Astoria, 65, 74, 128, 170, 181, 215
Astoria Riverwalk, 181
Audubon Society bird counts, 163

B

Bainbridge Island, 16, 55, 77, 179–180
Ballard, 51
Ballard Locks, 64, 78–79, 111
Bamfield, 62
Bandon, 114
beach camping trips, 16–19, 21
beach casting for salmon, 89–90
beach fires. *See* fires, open
beach hikes. *See* hiking
beach monitoring, 55, 112
beach projects
    beach volcano, 46
    beachside shade, 49
    beachside shelter hot dog roast, 155
    collected stardust, 48
    driftwood fort, *198*, 199
    fish prints, 100, *101*
    gear for kids' activities, 48
    gold-painted seashell ornaments, 151
    herbed sea salt, 97, 99
    lavender sea salt body scrub, 196
    message in a bottle, 200
    rock cairns, *98*, 99
    sand candles, 47
    sea-glass votive, *152*, 153–154
    seashell night-light, 197
    seashore fossils, 96
    walnut wish boats, 160, *161*
beachcombing, 154, 212
beaches for clamming, 25–26, 146–147
beaches for oyster harvesting, 190
beaches for surfing, 103, 105–106
beaches with tide pools, 208–212
beachside family reunions, 107–110
Bellingham, 7, 115
bike rides, 21–22
    day trips, 175–181
    gear and tips, 72
    multiday trips, 69–74
    nighttime, 65
    train hopping, 74
biking challenge, 179
bioluminescence viewing, 54–55
bird counts, 163
bird watching, 78, 163–164, 178
blackberries, 43–45, *44*, *45*
Blake Island, 10–12, *11*, 15
boating, 140, 201–206
    classes and education, 201–202, 206, 223
    nautical terms, 203
    nighttime tours, 53–54
    salmon fishing, 84, 85–87, 89
    sharing and rentals, 70, 181, 202, 204–206
    whale-watching trips, 3, 6–7
    See also kayaking; stand-up paddleboarding
boats, walnut wish, 160, *161*
bonfires. *See* fires, open
bottle, message in a, 200

About the Author

NANCY BLAKEY grew up on Bainbridge Island. She spent summers working for her family's salmon-processing business in Bristol Bay, Alaska, where she became an avid outdoor enthusiast who paddles, hikes, forages, and explores the great Pacific Northwest rain or shine, believing adventure can be found outside the back door year-round. She has written five children's activity books for Ten Speed Press and has contributed to numerous anthologies. She is the founder of the parenting website MudpieMamas.com.

Printed in China

Published by Sasquatch Books

22 21 20 19 18   9 8 7 6 5 4 3 2 1

Editor: Hannah Elnan | Production editor: Bridget Sweet
Copyeditor: Kirsten Colton | Design: Anna Goldstein
Photographs: Nick Hall | Illustrations: Teresa Grasseschi

ISBN: 978-1-63217-143-6

Sasquatch Books | 1904 Third Avenue, Suite 710 | Seattle, WA 98101
(206) 467-4300 | SasquatchBooks.com